Praise for **PERFECT DIRT**

"In *Perfect Dirt*, tenderness is so tangible, so electric. You feel it when a grandpa hoists a young Keegan Lester up so he can feed wild horses sugar cubes, you hear it when a grandma speaks thunder, it embraces you each time Lester holds close the good people of West Virginia. But this tenderness is also thorny: it sparks in the quiet togetherness of men, it leaps around a father lost at sea, it underscores loss and regret. Keegan Lester is an immensely gifted writer. This book will stay with you."

—Eduardo C. Corral, author of *Guillotine*

"Keegan Lester's writing and storytelling about West Virginia and its people feel how West Virginia's landscape feels to me—like I'm being hugged and protected. *Perfect Dirt* reminds us that we can love a place and still be critical when it's done out of love and tenderness. This book has brought me back home in the best ways, with a newer, more open heart, mind, and body."

—Steven Dunn, author of *water & power*

T0307932

PERFECT DIRT

AND OTHER THINGS I'VE GOTTEN WRONG

....

KEEGAN LESTER

....

WEST VIRGINIA UNIVERSITY PRESS • MORGANTOWN

Copyright © 2021 by West Virginia University Press
First edition published 2021 by West Virginia University Press
Printed in the United States of America

ISBN 978-1-952271-29-8 (paperback) / 978-1-952271-30-4 (ebook)

Library of Congress Control Number: 2021942333

Cover design by Emily Sokolosky / Co-owner, Base Camp Printing
Book design by Than Saffel / WVU Press

for my grandma

for my dad—big joe, bigs, and all the people you've been
and all the people you will become

contents

....

part one

part two

part three

part four

part five

part one

for all my strangers

....

We were listening to the bombing on the radio as my mother drove me to confirmation class. The radio said *We* as if America was a bunch of siblings who once shared a bed. The radio said *We* so someone could play the bombing over the radio and no one's feelings would get hurt. The radio said, *All Americans are We now, no matter what our differences once were.*

The radio said *We* are fighting terrorism in a place called Afghanistan. The radio said *We* will get them for what *they* did. The radio said *we're dropping bombs like thunder,* and I took offense because thunder is what happens before rain and rain's sacred to me.

The radio said *we've* started dropping bombs over cities in countries far, far away to fight a cell of terrorists in another country named Afghanistan and it made me wonder about all the things we do to others whose home we can't imagine in the soft ochre of our heads.

IT WAS October and my first year of high school and everything was changing.

The palm trees were slouching. First to the east and then the west. It must have been the Santa Ana winds blowing hard from the other side of the desert. Wind that started as a breath and a gust and dirt and sand from somewhere out near

Joshua Tree. It built up as it crossed mountain passes, picking
up pieces of the freeways and the suburbs until turning into a
fist. The fist of wind then turned into a pair of fists carrying
everything within its wind arms until it reached the Pacific.
It brought with it heat and breath and sand as it punched and
bruised the ocean with white caps.

And watching all those palm trees bend, I had to keep re-
minding myself that the bombing broadcasted over the radio
was not the thing moving the trees outside.

Wind. Wind. It's wind, I told myself every few minutes
as the howling fists of wind continued slamming against the
car and palm trees. *We're safe inside the car*, I kept telling
myself. I kept saying, *Wind is the thing making the other
things outside move.*

My mother and I were silent the whole drive, listening to
the broadcast of the bombs falling upon a place that then
neither of us yet knew how to properly imagine. A place existing in our minds as a place that could have been swapped for
any place that wasn't America.

As I walked into the confirmation meeting, the front door
ebbed open more than it was pulled by a human. It was as
if conjured by the invisible strings connected to an unseen
force, the way the moon tugs on the oceans with its gravity,
tugging on the door and on me. I could feel the strings pulling me into the living room, where every time I'd been before
we talked Jesus.

That night I felt the television before I saw it. I felt the television before I even got my shoes off at the doormat. I could
feel the others in the living room circling it. I couldn't help
but notice things.

I wasn't greeted at the door by cookies or the smile or the
pearls of the mother who had taken it upon herself to prepare
us for our spiritual journey. I was greeted by the gravity pulling at the strings that were all around us.

In the living room Raúl was sitting on the carpet leaning against an ottoman, his fist pumping at the television, making a gesture as if he'd just scored a touchdown. Laura wasn't crying. She wasn't smiling either. Her mouth made the mountain shape that mouths make when at rest. The abundance of lipstick on Julie's mouth, its slight smudge just beyond her lips made her mouth look like an open wound.

I couldn't keep from noticing all of it. Like Julie's crying. It wasn't the sad kind of crying. It's more the crying my grandfather talked about once.

....

My grandfather grew up in Morgantown, West Virginia. He grew up the kind of poor where he had to pull his father out of bars some nights in order to keep him from spending all the rent money. Because of that, my grandfather doesn't sit in bars.

Sometimes when we drive around South Park, one of the neighborhoods in town, he points out all the different places he moved in and out of.

"I lived in the white one on the corner of Greene Street, and that yella one over there and that one."

His sister liked football and basketball and thus decided the life of a nun was for her, and I've never once seen her drink anything in my life but the blood of Christ.

They lived the longest in a small house beneath a bridge on Pietro Street, next to some sort of factory with their father and a brother and their mother. Their mother was an Irish woman who loved God, bingo, and the parlay.

My dad, like me, loved his grandma very much. When he was still young and she was beginning to have trouble moving around, he would take her numbers down to the bar for her, like a good grandson.

"Hey Joe, what you up to?" a bartender would say to my seven- or eight-year-old father, on his way home from Mass.

"Just playing some numbers for Grandma."

"Alright boy, see you in a bit."

NOTHING CHANGES in Morgantown and like everything else, that bar is still there on the same street corner in South Park and you can still play the numbers if you want and an Irish woman tends the bar. Sometimes I'll grab a sheet of the parlay cards and wonder who my great-grandmother from Cork was.

Needless to say, my grandfather never went on vacations

as a child. He can't swim. He's still afraid of water and won't get close to it.

ABOUT SEVENTEEN years after he started walking, my grandfather started a family of his own. He worked on the tipple of a coal mine washing windows, a job he got because a friend of a friend knew he needed one. And after a few years of doing some more odd jobs inside and outside a coal mine, he started selling life insurance.

The first time he could afford to take a vacation, he took his family—my uncle Jimmy and my uncle Pat and my dad, Bigs, and my grandma—and packed them up tight in their station wagon and drove off in the middle of the night to Ocean City.

There was the usual fighting that happens between three young boys about distance: distance between locations, distance between the others' hands from their bodies, distance between their person and the stars, and the distance between facts and what they could prove with their bodies. And with my grandma, another kind of distance. Really all people ever argue about is distance. And after hours of this, his three boys and my grandma fell flat asleep.

The scatters of small towns along the highway must have looked to my grandpa like stars in distant galaxies where entire histories could be written and rewritten in the time it took to pass a town's highway exit. Each highway exit a door to a new and unknown world.

I like to think that he was sure someone was falling in love with someone else each time he passed a town. That someone was on the brink of dying, and another person about to be born. That someone was waking up, and the moonlight was piercing through the window on the naked body of a lover next to them in the bed they were sharing. That the naked sleeping body in the moonlight revealed something to the other who was awake. My grandpa struggled with sleep because in sleep people forget how to worry. He could never quite figure out how to keep himself from worrying. There was always too much to worry about. Too much to hide. Too much to do to waste on sleep.

That night, as he drove on, I like to think that he was sure some of the lovers in their beds had someone else waiting for them at home. Each cluster of light, town or burg, or highway exit he passed was another entrance to a foreign country with endless possibility and endless narrative.

Sometimes he talks about listening to AM radio when he was a boy. Catching signals from Pittsburgh and Cleveland and the beautiful narratives that actors were hired to play out.

"But you couldn't see nothing 'cause it was on the radio," he says.

Often, he remarks on how when he'd close his eyes and listen to all these beautiful narratives, all these beautiful people resembled people he knew. He cries when he tells me about such things.

The narratives always looked either like Morgantown or the Old West to him because that's all there was in the map of his brain. It was all he knew how to imagine back then. And these radio broadcasts were the only time he got to spend being young.

AND THAT night the sky peeled its blacks back. It turned to maroons and then into peaches and then to streaks of red.

I like to think of him pulling off to the side of the road as the others slept. Sneaking out of the car as quiet as he could and carefully wading out onto an unmarked beach. I like to think of him sitting and weeping there. These were *first time I've ever seen the ocean* tears.

I like to think of him as the Atlantic. A busted levee. How the ocean would have smelled to him nothing like the sea-salt taffy he chewed on as a child. How the sand he blanketed himself in was nothing like the sand on the banks of the Monongahela River and the creek beds of Decker's Creek, which were always flooding and leaving sand in places it shouldn't be. The banks smell of sulfur because the waterways are shared with coal barges and coal mines and with trains whistling at night taking their loads of coal to Pittsburgh.

This was different.

I like to think now on how the sounds of the ocean would have reminded him of the radio broadcasts from his youth, where a producer replicated sounds in a studio and *BANG BANG*, which was really just two pots banged together, might have stood in for thunder or a gunshot or a bar fight between two cowboys in the Old West. How the cacophony of these sounds transported him far, far away. Far from the place he lived. Far from his alcoholic father he'd drag home from bars. Far from the doom of a small life lived in his small town. Far from the coal barges and the coal trains whistling and the factory machinery bustling as he tried to sleep in his bed at night.

The Atlantic Ocean had its own sound. It was powerful. And there wasn't two pots in the whole world that could translate it. I like to think of him rolling up his pant legs and walking toward the ocean. Not quite into it as he was afraid of becoming ocean himself. He'd have let the ocean's fingertips come to him. He'd have let the water touch his toes and thought *No one talks about this foamy stuff after the water goes back into the ocean. I wonder why no one talks about what the ocean leaves behind?*

I like to think of him turning around and walking back to the car, not bothering to wake his wife or kids.

This was for him. This beach. The entire Atlantic. All of these tears were for him.

SCOTCH MAKES his eyes twinkle. They twinkle when he's been telling stories. It's the way I like to imagine the night sky twinkling above him that night, like all the towns and burgs

from the side of the highway as he came up with narratives
to help explain all of this that he was seeing for the first time.
How none of it was Morgantown or Fairmont or Thomas or
Charleston or nothing in West Virginia. It was a new map.

And I wonder what California must have looked like to
my father the first time he saw it, after he left West Virginia,
deciding to make a home somewhere else.

I like to think their eyes twinkled.

I like to think of my grandfather's eyes having something
in common with all these foreign places as he drove on and
on through the night, while his children were still young and
asleep without worry or understanding yet of the cruelty of
the world.

....

Julie's tears are like that.

Like whatever she's watching on the television screen is hers and only hers. Like no one else in the living room exists.

Frank's quietly cheering.

"Serves those fuckers right," Mark whispers to Matt.

IT WAS a time in US history when no matter what you said, if you whispered it, just by lowering your voice, you were absolved from the weight of what you said. This is how we were taught to be patriots in our living rooms.

In that living room in Southern California it was clear to everyone but me who the enemy was.

For the first time I see it. I see the television. The swarming green blurs. I wonder what the green blurs are. I wonder what their movements are supposed to signify.

A *whooooooooosh* of white flashes across the screen. The kind of white strobe of the fireworks I'd set off only a couple months earlier when it was still July and the humidity and night still innocent and the world not yet changed, and somehow we were all more related to each other back then, back in the days when *POP POP POP* still sounded like July and *POP* like January.

There are no sounds coming from the television. The blurs stop moving after the flashes. My mouth is a lake of cotton. Cotton rubbing cotton. There is friction, but no sound. Just dry sensations tingling neck and spine.

That was the first time I'd seen anyone die.

I was at a Catholic confirmation meeting in the late fall of 2001 and I had just started high school and was fourteen and the younger George Bush was president. And people all around me were celebrating.

I'd seen people get blown up in movies and video games. I'd altar-served some three hundred funerals. I'd seen pictures of

Anne Frank and soldiers of Antietam and Gettysburg, their
mouths looking like blowfish. But they were never living to
me. I never saw their movements before the pose that would
eternalize their bodies in those pictures. Black and white
never makes the images look like I could have shared a world
with those in the images.

I can't understand Laura's mouth turning up into a smile. I
sort of understand Raúl's fist pumping *U-S-A, U-S-A, U-S-A*.

RAÚL WAS adopted by rich white people. The kind of rich
white people who shop for their children from magazines
while sitting in first class on their way home from a vacation
to an island off the coast of Central America where the Spanish name sounds right, but the translation makes one realize
that it has no semblance to the place because it was a name
given to people by their conquerors, by their colonizers.

More than anything, Raúl wanted his parents. Secondly,
he wanted people to see him the way he saw himself. Like the
others and also different. This is what I wanted people to see
in me too, to see in West Virginia and in my family.

. . . .

One time in middle school during science class we watched a movie called *October Sky* about a West Virginia boy named Homer Hickam who wins a medal for learning to shoot rockets really well in high school, even though he had to quit high school and work in a coal mine for a spell because his father was injured. And because he knew he wasn't big enough to play football and wasn't going to be able to get a scholarship as a water boy—as none of the thousands of remarkable children born in coal camps in West Virginia would get football scholarships and would eventually die in their dying coal camp, in or outside a coal mine that was dying too—one day he said, *Yeah, fuck it, let's try rocket science. I mean how hard can it be?*

At this point in time, this was the only movie in the history of movies with anything nearing a kind portrayal of West Virginia. So I'd seen it hundreds of times.

"Now this takes place in Western Virginia," my science teacher said.

I raised my hand.

"Yes, Keegan."

"No, it takes place in West Virginia. You're thinking of a different state."

A student behind me snickered. "She's the teacher. I think she'd know if West Virginia was a state or not."

WORSE THAN the stereotypes I've heard people utter about the place and about people from the place, often by people who call themselves liberal or conservative or progressive or whatever it is they think fit to call themselves, was when someone spoke as if the place didn't exist.

You can debate and argue a stereotype, but how do you explain the existence of a place to someone? How do you explain to someone who doesn't believe you that my grandma exists. My grandpa exists. My dad and my uncles and cousins, they exist too. My heart exists.

....

And so I warn you now, as you read on, I am not the protago-
nist. I'm part villain and part lover, like you. Part dreamer
and part optimist. I'm also lost and stumbling but trying to
find my way back.

I was certain the night I watched bombs falling over Afghanistan and Pakistan on television that there were children
in those places who didn't want to go to school the next day
and some who did. I was certain someone in Afghanistan
wanted to be an astronaut and looked out at the sky the way
Homer Hickam looked out into the sky over West Virginia
and saw Sputnik, knowing they wanted to shoot rockets,
knowing they wanted a chance to make a life. I was certain
it would be the kids in West Virginia, my family, my people,
who would be tasked with going to Afghanistan and Iraq
and Pakistan to fight. And they were. It's always the people
from places in America who other Americans don't want
who get tasked with having to kill people in other places for
Americans who don't want to go, who want to call themselves
patriots for hating strangers from their living room, strangers who I have more in common with than most Americans.

I was certain that night that my people would be asked
to kill strangers who just wanted to be in love and wanted
to go to school or play hooky from school or become astro-
nauts, just like them. I don't know the names or ages of the
deceased, but I'm sure that some of them were just getting
born and others were falling in love. Some were bad people
and some were good and most were both. Some had to drag
their fathers home down dark alleys because if they didn't
their fathers would spend the family's rent money. I was sure
that someone was having their first kiss because the sky was
falling. I was sure that as the sky fell, someone knew they
would never be lovers with someone else because the sky was
falling and this kiss would have to be enough.

And *enough* for the first time in history had to be enough because, though their life was precious, it was being taken from them.

And so in a living room thousands of miles from the flashes on the television screen, I thought of strangers kissing as the sky fell all about them.

welch

....

I was wearing short shorts the first time I went down to McDowell County because I only had one pair of shorts at the time and it was hot and they were short and the whole drive down I thought, *Man, I'm gonna get my ass kicked.*

The road squeezed the mountains like a lover, and like a lover, sometimes the roads forsook those mountains. Those roads were built to take these mountains and trees in pieces from this state to another.

When we got far enough south, all roads became one way in and one way out. Then a thick tree canopy like a shroud keeping what's enchanted in its place. The dark and wet greens swaddling us from the world. Rain poured from clouds we couldn't see. The car windows were rolled down and we could hear the rain in the trees, but the water was unable to sneak its way through, and the windshield remained untouched and I thought, *I'm gonna get my ass handed to me when we get to Welch.*

A FEW days ago it was West Virginia Day and my friend, who I had not seen in nearly four years, and I had been drinking at the fancy bar beneath my apartment. And like everyone else, we were so full of West Virginia pride.

"Wanna go to Welch in a few days to see *The Hollow Project* premier?" she asked.

"Yeah, but I don't know how I'm going to get down there," I said.

"I'll drive back up and pick you up," she said.

And a few days later, my friend who I'd not seen in nearly four years drove two hours out of her way—from Charleston all the way up to Morgantown in the northern part of the state—just to turn around and drive us to the most southern part. People from here are like that. West Virginians will do almost anything in the name of West Virginia or for another West Virginian.

ON THE drive down to Welch, as everything turned green and more green and then spooky green and then damp, my friend and I talked about leaving the state for school and work and coming back. About how I felt bad sometimes for forgetting the way the moon here grins. How the water baptizes you if you swing into it from a tree. How beer cans float in swimming holes next to their human like little tugboats. How people here sing sometimes for no reason at all, just to sing.

Even when I leave West Virginia physically, I'm never able to mentally leave the place. I wear it like a birthmark. And like a birthmark, it's this part of me that I love and sometimes feel different for. It's a thing the people who love me love me for and strangers often feel a thing that should be covered up or talked about in a singular way. Through a singular lens.

But like anything else in life, place and home are more complicated than just a single lens.

THE HOLLOW *Project* is an experimental documentary about population decline and brain drain in the southern part of the state. There had at one point been a hundred thousand people living in Welch and now there's only about twenty-two thousand left.

Welch at one time was one of the richest cities in America. When coal left so did most of the people. Because the land's topography changed, trees taken for lumber and mountains blown away for coal, the town started flooding all the time. After about three floods back people said, "I guess we just gonna leave it like this, 'cause no one lives here." But people do live there and if you go, you'll see.

You'll see a city that was once majestic. You'll see a theater and its marquee like a crown filled with jewels. Glamorous architecture and the excess of the 1950s. Flat iron–shaped buildings and everything two stories and up that the floods did not smudge, looking as if they were from another time completely. Welch is a time machine that way.

Pretty much everyone in McDowell and Logan County who wanted to say something in front of those cameras said something. There were folks who were musicians and folks who liked to four-wheel and folks in the armed services, including a general, and folks who taught children to read and write and folks who grew gardens to feed those children because there isn't always enough to go around and folks who mine coal and folks who used to mine coal. There were folks of all colors and creeds and sexual orientations and that's something that no one mentions about West Virginia, that all of these different kinds of folks live here too. And for the first time in history, they all got to just sit in front of a camera talking about what they love.

Like one guy said, *I love four-wheeling,* and another said, *I love my grandparents*, and another said, *I love being the mascot for the high school football team.* Just by the way the fog seeped into the trees around the field, spilling out of the mountains as he danced in his pirate costume, as if he was the one conjuring the fog and conjuring the town to this field and conjuring the kids exploding through time and space on the field, I believed he did love being the mascot.

Some talked about what they've lost and their hopes for their children.

And there was so much footage that all the videos ended

up just standing on their own. It was one documentary, but also an entire library of home movies where you could pick and choose which ones you wanted and which you needed and there was so much to discover.

Elaine Sheldon, who'd grown up in Logan County, West Virginia, called it an interactive documentary. It was the first time I can think of when people in West Virginia got to be in a film where they just said what they were feeling and were allowed to be all the different and complicated things that make us human. For once they weren't just one thing but were allowed to be people telling stories.

And people telling stories is how I came to fall in love with West Virginia as a young child on my grandpa's porch.

No one beat me up in Welch. One person said, "You look skinny. Let me get you cornbread and some fixings." My friend said, "When I left West Virginia for college, I spent two years trying to forget how my mother talked." She said, "Like this town, though, no matter what happens to you, some part of you stays the same." She said, "I kept looking for home everywhere but here. But I'm home now."

So if you have to leave West Virginia someday too, don't forget the cornbread and the food pantries from the gardens that locals in Welch keep so school kids have something to eat when there isn't enough to go around. Don't forget Welch or Parkersburg or Keyser or Jane Lew or Ridgewood.

When you enter downtown Welch, there's a mural that a guy just started painting one day because he had to, because sometimes your heart forces you to translate beauty for others. And just by looking at his painting, you can tell how full his heart is with this place.

Sometimes beauty is someone inviting you into their home.

....

I've been told I won't understand the chatter of foxes at night because I wasn't born here and it's not my magic to be had. Though, sometimes, someone here leaves an extra plate of food out for you anyway, for no reason at all other than you look skinny. We don't always get to choose how magic tugs on us.

a snapshot

....

In the city I grew up in, there was no glimpse of West Virginia. There was no place to eat the food that my father was raised on. There was no one who spoke like my grandma or grandpa or believed in magic or the improbable. There were no trains whistling at night or woods that whispered their secrets.

My father would wake me up at seven in the morning Saturdays in the fall from the time I was eight or so and we'd call all the bars in our city and neighboring cities to see if anyone had the West Virginia University football game on through a satellite feed. Then he'd take me to a bar and we'd eat chicken wings at nine in the morning. While all the surfers were out surfing and the people who brunched weren't even awake yet, and while skaters dreamed their ethereal dreams, we watched our giants run into other giants through a grainy television screen and my dad would get choked up on beer and tell me a little bit about being a boy in Morgantown.

My father is my father but once he was only Joseph. Then he was Joe, then Fatty, then he grew into a redwood of a man and was renamed Bigs. Then he grew into all these other people and one day he turned thirty-two and a month and some change, and he became my father and now he's my father and Big Joe because I know his secrets.

My mother was born Kathleen and grew up Kathy in South

Florida. Stunningly beautiful her whole life. She was a class president and a prom queen and once someone took a picture of her while she was jogging and they put it on billboards. Then she became a nurse and took care of babies who were born too small during the crack epidemic, babies who were too sick to live on and, despite everything dying does to the body, she'd tell these babies *you must continue on, you must live on, you're meant to live on* and she would hold these babies in her reed basket arms, telling them she loved them, long after everyone else had gone to sleep. *You are loved* and *you are loved* and *you are loved.* And sometimes she named the babies. And some nights I imagine her sitting up in bed looking out at the night sky recalling names of these babies she named until running out of stars in the Western Hemisphere. And one day she drove across America until she arrived on a beach shouldering the Pacific. And a few years later she became *Mom.*

And then I was one of the babies born too small.

AND SO I was raised by these people in a place that was like neither of the places they came from, and I never took to the language of the place where I was raised.

SOMETIMES I like to imagine my father moving from West Virginia to Colorado to California. I imagine everyone telling him *forget*. And I imagine him closing his eyes, trying to forget. I imagine him taking his clothes off, putting new clothes on, and then opening his eyes as someone whispers to him *Forget everything you've ever known if you want to be one of us.*

Forget hot dogs and pepperoni rolls and birch leaves turning colors and forget the snow. Forget the way the seasons turn slow like honey from a spoon. Forget the people you gave your shoes away to up the hill in Osage and forget what's left of those coal camps. Forget all the lawns you mowed summer after summer so you could afford to study abroad in Paris during high school, so you could learn to bake bread and drink wine from stolen wine jugs. And forget the giant French flag you stole from a ferry in France and brought home and hung in your basement. Forget your basement. Forget how small the town you came from is. Forget wanting to major in political science in college, dreaming of going to law school, and instead majoring in coal mine engineering because the local coal companies paid the scholarships of children from West Virginia, children who they could get to put their dreams on hold for a hole in the ground that one day, one way or another, would end them. Forget South High Street and the cemetery at the end of South High Street filled to the brim with bodies. Forget all those bodies and forget how when walking through that cemetery the unleveled ground feels like small bony fists beneath your shoes. Forget cutting through the cemetery when you were late for school, the dead you had to walk over if you were to succeed. Forget the Mon River cutting the hills away from each other and forget the coal mines and the trains pulling their small children train cars full of coal from your hills upriver to Pittsburgh or Ohio to the people who would make fun of your accent and ask if you wear shoes, if you could read and then who built their stadiums and museums and universities with money from the backs of the people and landscapes you love, that are part of you like a scar. And forget your grandfather came to this country from Lithuania, how when your people tried to form unions the United States army fired upon them. Forget that your grandpa only went to school to the third grade but could do statistics. Forget how in spite of all of that, he would one day become the mayor of his coal camp. Forget your grandfather. Forget your grandfather came to this country from Lithuania. Forget the boat your grandfather came over on, the banana he ate whole, because he'd never seen a banana before and didn't know to peel it. And forget those trains carrying coal, whistling at night, whistling *Joe Joe Joe Joe Joe*, and forget the way your name sounds in the mouth of those hills and streams and beneath the rocks you used to collect. Forget your rock collection. Forget how when you left West Virginia, you left with nearly nothing but this collection of rocks.

WHILE MY father changed a little, trying his damnedest, he found that he could only be who he could be.

············

You ever been so lost you forget where you're from? Like you
just wake up one morning and you've been out at sea too long
or in a mountain listening to streams running all streamy
over some rocks or underbrush for so long, you forget the
way your name sounds in the mouth of your own mother, the
way it sounded when she yelled [fill in your name] and you
yelled back *am I in trouble?* and she yelled *nooooooo.* But
now you're in trouble for forgetting the way your mother's
voice sounds, for forgetting your native tongue, for stealing
someone else's tongue and making it your own. That's my
problem. With no native tongue, I worry I'm from nowhere.

cardinals staining the air we breathe

....

"I'm still not sure she wanted to marry me," Grandpa says.

Tap tap tap.

His fingers keep time on the dining room table. He's gotten good at pacing himself as he tells his stories. There's a music in his head that only he can hear. I've heard this story hundreds of times during my seven years of living and know it by heart.

"She didn't even hold my hand at the practice the night before the wedding," he says. He pauses. He cranks his neck around from his newspaper at the dining table to look into the kitchen.

"I wasn't sure I wanted to marry you, James," my grandma says, walking to the table with a fresh deck of cards.

He looks at her with a look that I've always taken to be a knowing of secret holding. The kind of look that says *I know you love me and that's why we're married and have been married for fifty-something years and we don't even need to say it anymore because some things are alright left unsaid.*

I might have only been seven at the time but I understood the look.

"She didn't even kiss me when I let her out of the car at the house after the wedding rehearsal. Did I ever tell you about fighting for hours and hours with her dad to convince him to let me marry her? He's just as strong headed as her and a mean cuss."

"My dad was a smart man," she says.

"She's a pony without a saddle. That's what her father said about her."

And the look she shoots him, I swear, is love, is the kind of look I've never seen anyone shoot anyone with. Not my mother or my father or my cousins or their parents or the people acting on television or in the movies. But I'm only seven, so I'd never been in love before. Maybe I'm not the most expert on what the telltale signs are.

My grandmother shuffles the deck of cards.

"Cut it."

I cut it two-thirds down. I watch her perform magic on the cards. She bridges with the sleight of hand of windmills. The cards fold into each other and then away from each other and then halt.

"Now I'll keep score," she says. "You remember gin rummy, right, Keegan?"

"Don't trust her with numbers," Grandpa says.

....

My parents are far away in California, and West Virginia reeks of summer and the thunder rolls in before the rain comes and goes and in the morning when my grandpa thumbs his rosary, mornings where I can stand to get up early enough, we watch cardinals dart through the porch. I watch the flowers open and jockey for position to catch the rain. I watch the flowers reach toward where they think the sun will appear later in the day as if from muscle memory. I watch the fire station a block or so down the street which stays silent. I watch the synagogue across the street which is silent and foreign and beautiful, a single light in the front. I think of the time my cousins huddled behind the safety of the bricks of our porch and waited for cars to make their slow approach from the High Street Bridge: *WoooooooOO OOOOOoooooooooooooooOOOOWoooooooooooooooo oooooooooooooooooooooo oooooooooo*, they moaned as loud as they could, mimicking a firetruck or police car at the oncoming vehicle. "Dad taught us how to do that," they said. And sometimes the vehicle would slow down or stop before they realized no one was around. That it must have been teen pranksters or ghosts. And those mornings where I'd pull myself out of bed at five and sit with my grandpa on the porch, him in the recliner and me on the porch swing glider with blankets wrapping us, I would think about us being ghosts. I would think about how everything I knew came from here, and from the looks my grandma and grandpa shot each other with. How everything I knew came from the cardinals staining the air around us red. I knew they stained the air with their bodies, air that could not have been sky, because humans don't go into the sky except on airplanes, but still the same air that we share with the cardinals that they fly through. I never knew what that word was or if there was a word for it, the way that I'd get confused that the ocean is both a body of water with a surface where things can be seen and also a depth so large that we could never fathom seeing everything in its reach. How come there wasn't another word for that? How come there wasn't a word for the different kinds of ocean and different kinds of sky? The one all around us that we walk through and the one above us? The one we reach for? I'd think about all of this in the early black summer mornings on the porch next to my grandfather as he prayed the rosary and I watched fingers of lightning peel black sky to blue sky to red.

············

"Don't trust her with numbers," Grandpa says.

I LOOK UP from the card game.

"Did I ever tell you about the time in Buckhannon where she was working the concession stands at the high school football game and was giving too much change and not enough change, but your grandma was so beautiful she could get away with it," he says.

My grandma looks at him again with another look, that for every year of my life I'd mistook for love.

AND THAT night when I went to sleep, I was watching the lightning in the sky above the synagogue across the street. I was watching lighting in the sky above the hills across the bridge into Westover, lightning in the sky for miles and miles above the wild, and I listened to the trains whistle through the wild, carrying their coal to Pittsburgh. And I was thinking about how beautiful I'll have to become one day to be like my grandmother, who's the keeper of her own rules.

shane rooney

....

is the only person I've ever known other than Adrian's grandmother who's died. And on account that my grandmas live across the country, while she was still alive, Adrian let me borrow his grandma from time to time on grandparents' day at our school. She was good to me. She spoke no English but smiled like my grandma smiles and smelled like my grandmother smells and I'd only met her three or four times, but the last time I saw her I was altar-serving her funeral and tripped on my robe and fell down the flight of steps leading to the altar. But I don't think anyone saw me because when I said, "Adrian, I'm sorry," and he said, "For what?" and I said, "For tripping down a flight of stairs while altar-serving your grandmother's funeral," he just said "Oh," like he didn't see me.

SHANE ROONEY was on my peewee football team. He wasn't much bigger than me, but he hit a ton harder and was younger and had a future and was fearless. I never knew if it was because his dad had been to jail before and he knew at any moment he'd have to be the man in his house if called upon. It's hard to know at that age.

I was thirteen and had to put fishing weights in my pockets during the weigh-ins at tryouts and I still didn't make weight and so had to play in a lower division below my age group with

the eleven-year-olds. And even then I was small. Officially I
was called an older-lighter.

Our coach, coach Brown, was not very good at coaching
football.

Day one he looked at all the kids and the families at the
parent family barbecue and he sighed. "We're not going to
win very many games this year," he said.

And I believed him.

We all looked at each other mouthing, *What?* I pretended
to be in disbelief, but we were really small and young and
then Coach Brown said, *But that's okay.*

And I thought, *Great.*

I remember, as the older-lighter on the team, most of the
reason I was a starter was because I understood concepts and
schemes the others didn't get, mostly because I was thirteen
and they were ten. Sometimes before practice, if I got there
a little early, Coach would be sitting on the practice field
smoking a cigarette and I'd say, *Hey, Coach*, and he'd look
at me, his eyes all glassy for reasons I would not understand
until years later, and he would say, "Lester, a woman ever
made you cry?"

Looking back, I'm pretty sure Coach was stoned. But at
the time I thought, *This must be a test.* I thought, *The only
women I know are all the teachers I've ever had, nuns, and
my mom.*

"Not yet, Coach," I lied.

"Great, don't let it happen."

I thought, *Wow, this guy has some grown-man problems*,
a phrase I once overheard my older cousin say. And sometimes Coach would tell me about his grown-man problems
as we waited for the ten- and eleven-year-old kids to show up
for practice, ferried in by their mothers in a minivan armada.

At the time I didn't even consider asking myself why this
crazy old man was talking about losing his woman and child
and not being able to make rent or pay child support to a

thirteen-year-old kid he coaches. At the time I was thinking, *Wow I must be a super wise older-lighter.*

AGAINST ALL odds we even won a game that year.

Every time I strapped my helmet on and bit down into my mouthpiece I thought *I'm gonna die, I'm gonna die, I'm gonna die.* But sometimes everything would be moving so fast I'd forget about my fear of dying on the football field and just do my job. Usually those were the best moments of my career.

Shane Rooney on the other hand, when he put his helmet on and bit into his mouthpiece, he was a superhero. He made just about every tackle our team logged that year. He flew all over the field like a chicken with its head cut off and often I wonder how fearless I could be if I could learn to separate my head from my heart and just fly like him.

....

Sometimes I catch a glimpse of my street's lamppost light through my window and I think about angels and I think about God and how lonely winter can be. I think about the time after a scrimmage, my dad walked me back to his Astro van and said, "I'm never gonna watch you play football again unless you make a hit."

I'd like to think my dad was trying to motivate me to be less scared. But I also know it would be pretty embarrassing to have been my dad. To have to take time off from work to come see your son get run over on the football field, over and over. Everyone on the team was terrible, but I found new and creative and almost innovative ways to suck on the football field.

The next scrimmage, I was no longer starting. I stood on the sideline and waited. I was thinking and waiting. I was waiting and thinking. I was thinking I better do something or my dad's never gonna come see me again.

The very first play they put me in I entered the game thinking at thirteen this might be my last chance to win my father's love.

I played corner and had to cover a wide receiver who was much bigger than me. The other team's coach saw me and how small I was. He yelled *TIME OUT* and ran out on the field and changed up the play. And the coach pointed right at me. As if I couldn't see him. As if my team and my dad couldn't see him do it. He was like, *Run at that little guy.*

Then a big eleven-year-old kid was given the ball and ran right at me thinking *I'm way bigger than that guy.* And he was right.

But I buried my helmet in his knee. *CRAAAACK.*

The bone in his knee broke and I could feel it splinter. My eyes were wide open as it happened and everyone on my sideline cheered as the eleven-year-old boy on the field was unable to get up. My dad was screaming, *That's my boy.* My coach was screaming *There you go, Lester.* The big eleven-year-old kid was screaming too and his dad came out on the field like he was Daedalus telling Icarus to get up and walk out of the ocean.

Try as that boy did, he couldn't.

And I was named player of the game that night. And I wasn't afraid anymore.

Sometimes I think about that *crack*. I think about how so much of our happiness and progress and understanding of ourselves comes at the expense of others or something else. I hear that *crack* often when I'm by myself at night, when I'm all alone with my thoughts and I think it's just me. And each time it's just as jarring as the first.

. . . .

In the newspaper article about how my friend Shane Rooney was killed, his teachers all agree that he was an energetic boy, housing a ton of charisma. The newspaper said *The seventh grader was active in local youth sports, including Little League and Pop Warner football*, and according to the newspaper the accident was not the first that Shane encountered.

According to a February 8, 2001, article in the *LA Times*,

> About a month [before Shane died, he] survived another alleged drunk driving accident on the way to a weekend competition in Needles, near the Arizona border. Barrett Brown, a 35-year-old Pee Wee coach for the city's Pop Warner football chapter, was arrested by the California Highway Patrol after his 1995 Isuzu Rodeo overturned on a highway Dec. 1, five miles outside the California city, authorities said.
>
> Brown . . . was carrying three boys between 11 and 12 years old, to a postseason football game in Laughlin, Nev. Shane had slipped out of his seat belt and was thrown through the window of the sport utility vehicle after the glass popped out. Brown and the three boys suffered bruises and scratches. No one was seriously hurt in the accident. They were treated at Needles Desert Communities Hospital and released that day.

. . . .

The temperature would have been in the upper eighties and saguaro would have been blooming yellow and pink, and yellow and pink would have been smeared everywhere, all around Shane. And the air would have been painted thick with dust as he, the smallest of the boys in the car, after being ejected, ran a mile and a half down the shoulder of highway until finding help for the others.

Every day for the rest of his life after that, people called him "hero," though he'd been protecting us long before that. After Shane had been called hero by his neighbors and teachers and friends, and hero by strangers he never met, and hero by the mothers of the boys he found help for, he was hit by a drunk driver while standing with his scooter on a sidewalk in front of his house.

I don't know if I believe Fate always comes for us. Though, storytelling sometimes makes more bearable the fact that we are the ones left behind to live on after the story we remember. I also don't not think Fate comes for us either.

But I like to remember the POP Shane made when making contact, an M-80 causing everyone on the sideline to jolt back. I like to remember how he didn't know anything when I knew him because he was only ten years old and the funeral home where his wake was, was next door to a Condom Revolution sex shop, and I like to remember that so some part of us can smile, as Shane would have smiled at the word *sex* and *condom* because when he died he was twelve and didn't know better. The other boys on the team then didn't know any better and I didn't know better either. And I like to think of it so all of us that don't know any better can smile for a moment. And I like remembering the life of a child who could hit you so hard you shit blood for a week, who also may have still believed in Santa Claus.

the way in which wind moves

....

Senior year in high school I was supposed to work all year on an English project. A little bit every day of every week. All year long. I was supposed to define words like *alliteration* and *simile* and *dramatic irony,* and *a hundred and fifty others,* citing passages from the works we read over the year including Byron, Joyce, Beckett, Woolf in addition to some other rich dead white guys.

Up until my senior year I had been in regular English. I liked books and English class, but it was boring.

Sometimes I thought, *All we do in this class is read the diaries of dead people.* Sometimes I thought, *Not everything an author wrote was supposed to be a metaphor for Terrorism or McCarthyism.* One time I said aloud, *Not everything is supposed to be a metaphor for something else. I think this writer just wanted to tell a story.*

But try as I did, my teacher kept saying, "Trust me. This means this other thing." And that other thing was never on the page.

"Then why didn't the writer just write that?" I asked one day, and this was enough for my teacher to suggest that I take AP English my senior year to avoid us having the chance of taking another class together, and like an idiot I said, "Alright, I like books."

Week one, when I got the syllabus, I planned silently in my head how I would work little by little to finish all of it on schedule. I had a stack of books and I thought, *I'm going to love this. I love books.* Then my teacher said, "And I'm going to hold you accountable to finish all of this on your own over the year." She paused a second and then continued, "In college no one is going to be there to help you keep deadlines."

And I thought, *Alright.*

INSTEAD OF doing what I had planned on doing in my head all those weeks ago, I did what seniors do: I listened to emo music, got good and depressed about the one time in life when there was not much to be depressed about, and I procrastinated. I procrastinated and procrastinated and procrastinated and was forced to finish a thirty-two-week project in five and a half weeks of going to school, going straight home, drinking coffee and working until five in the morning and sleeping an hour, drinking more coffee and doing it again six days a week for five weeks straight until I was crapping blood.

I'm still not sure what that was about, the crapping blood part, but it wasn't good and I'd never told anyone any of this until now, especially the part about the crapping blood.

THE NIGHT I finished the project, it was early morning and my parents had left earlier that day with my younger sister on a trip to Las Vegas. I didn't know what to do. I thought on it for a second and decided, *I'm gonna go do something grown up.* So I hopped into my car and went to a gas station to buy candy and a pack of Black and Mild cigars to celebrate, like an idiot.

My car heater was blasting because it was in the fifties, which is cold in Southern California, and my hoodie was snug tight around my head, and a little after four in the morning I strolled into the gas station, having not slept more than twenty hours a week for the last five weeks, drinking too much coffee and crapping blood, and I said, "Can I get a pack of Black and Milds and these Snickers bars?"

The attendant looked at me for a second and then turned to the wall of cigarettes, grabbed the pack and put it on the checkout counter. "Anything else?"

"Nope."

"Alright, dude. Seven dollars and eighty-five cents."

That was easy.

WALKING OUT the store and back into my car I think about a kid named Jeremy that I grew up with, how he's now in prison for robbing this very gas station. Jeremy was one of the foster kids from down the street, and his foster brother Jake who was his foster mom's biological son was older than us and used to take us biking in this secret place called Sheep Hills that became less of a secret as our town grew into the tourist destination it is now. Jake taught me to throw a football and when I learned to do a pop-wheelie, I flew down the street like the wind to show him and I said, *Hey, look at this trick I learned,* and he told me, *No real man does a trick on a bicycle with training wheels*, so I went home and took my training wheels off that day and practiced falling off my bike. And Jake was my hero. When Jake told me flag football wasn't real football, I signed up for tackle the next season. This one time Jake and his biological brother Michael, who used to tutor me in math and computers when I was younger, said, *Hey, Keegan, eat this. There's chocolate in the middle.*

AT THE time I was seven and the people I looked up to said there was chocolate in the middle of a dog treat.

So I took a bite.

There was no chocolate in the middle of the dog treat. I mean now I know that chocolate would have killed a dog, but I didn't know that then. I was just so desperate for chocolate because it was scarce in my household, because my mom was like, *you will not be one of those kids* 60 Minutes *is always talking about with the diabetes and a Nintendo.* Jake called it a *Nofriendo*, so I've never been much of a gamer. This other time Jake had to clean his room up and he had all this neat stuff inside like stickers and hockey sticks and a boomerang from Australia and I said, *If you're throwing out that sticker can I have it?* and he said *well sure, but you have to take everything.* So after carrying four loads of stuff in my small seven-year-old arms out of his room down the stairs and down the block to my house and up my staircase into my room, after four of those trips later, I had the sticker.

As I sit in my car waiting for it to heat up, I'm thinking about how Jake was popular in high school and a great athlete and about a day when his foster brother Jeremy and another kid and I were playing football and Jake was playing with us and the foster kid hit someone incorrectly and Jake said, *Jeremy, if you do that again I'm done with you,* and I'm not sure Jeremy was bad intentioned, but I'm very sure that he wasn't very smart. And that's coming from a guy who ate a dog treat hoping there would be chocolate in the middle. I like to think of Jeremy most of the time as a light. He was always very sweet, but he just couldn't keep himself from doing stupid shit. He'd become infamous for saying, *perfect dirt*, when trying to describe a landing zone at the end of a dirt bike jump to my cousin from West Virginia. My cousin pulled me aside and said, *Is this guy dicking me around because I'm from West Virginia?* I said, *No, that's just Jeremy.* As the day wore on, *perfect dirt* became more an explanation for Jeremy than a description for a landing zone for a bike jump. We used to talk about Jeremy searching for dirt the way surfers chase waves and the summer, which now almost makes Jeremy seem ambitious. It sounded dumber back then than it does now, I guess. I guess he could see the importance and beauty in something that we couldn't. Someone is always trying to convince us of beauty in what we can't see. But the day we were playing football, Jeremy tackled another kid the same way he was told not to by Jake and, like I said, not because he intended to hurt the kid but because he's dumb and Jake walked away from the game and shouted, *I'm done with you,* and he was done with all of us that afternoon. It wasn't long after that his brother Michael made the largest drug bust in the history of our town. People thought he was crazy for turning in all that money and drugs, which were just sitting out all unattended in a car by the beach. He could have been set up for life, but that was the way Michael was. Just doing the right thing no matter what, aside from the time he tricked me into eating a dog treat. Before he was the famous cop that made the largest drug bust in our town's history, and before he became a cop, he taught me to surf and was a lifeguard in the summer and tried to get me to be less terrified of the ocean any way he could. But try as he did, I was terrified of the ocean.

After that football game, Jake stopped talking to Jeremy and after a high school breakup, he stopped talking to all of us, and it was the worst breakup I'd ever heard of. I think I heard the girl that broke up with him started dating Mark McGuire who was an MLB baseball player on steroids at the time and had a home run record. Even though Jake was my hero, I don't know how you compete with that. I overheard someone drunk years later say, *McGuire's penis must have been the size of a pinky after all those steroids.* I think the whole thing was more about the magic of first love and less about the penis size of Mark McGuire, but it's hard to tell. What did I know? I was nine or ten then. Jake kind of disappeared after that and I wasn't sure if it was from getting hit in the head too many times in football or from a broken heart, or if he'd just always been that way. But Jeremy and I were just kids. We didn't know all the telltale signs, as kids who look up to their heroes never think of them as breakable or people, just the beings that tower over us, that capture our intrigue and imagination.

And then one day I heard that Michael, the most famous cop in our town, shot and killed a man. He was entering a home while on duty and a mentally ill man raised a gun at him while he was trying to talk and Michael fired. And like all things Michael did, Michael fired well and he killed the man. The man's gun wasn't a real gun. And after that Michael stopped being able to sleep at night. He couldn't be much of a cop after that, because sometimes even cops need to sleep. So he went to nursing school and became a nurse, which fit him better. I don't know why we don't tell our young boys who want to make their communities better, who are honest and strong and fearless, to become nurses. I think if we did we'd have a different world all together. One day Michael got a dog and it was his everything. And all I know of him now is that he's a nurse with a dog, who's a good human, who taught me to surf and doesn't sleep at night anymore, who taught me math and computers and told me not to be afraid of the ocean, no matter how deep and dark and infested with sharks and stingrays it may be and like his brother Jake, he's quiet now too. And I wonder if that's part of getting older. That you become quiet. That getting older just means you hold all these things that have broken you, inside you, and the only way to keep them still, to keep your body intact, is by being quiet.

WHILE I sit in my car waiting for it to warm, I think about how Jeremy had a girlfriend and how I met her this year in a photography class and she was the only person kind to me in that class and the only person that talked to me in that class and we'd talk about how we both missed Jeremy, who was sitting in jail for robbing this very gas station. And in the car I think about how a friend of mine attempted to end her life a few weeks ago and that's why I started focusing on my English project, that I was trying to fix the thing broken in me hoping it might save both of us, that if I could just get to college, get to West Virginia, that everything would be OK. And at night before bed I'd pray to God, I'd say, *God, If you help me get out of here and get to West Virginia, where I know everything will be OK, I'll do anything.* And when I wasn't praying for that I was praying that everything for everyone would be OK, and because my father's friend had just killed himself a few months prior to that and my friend had just tried to kill herself and everyone seemed to be dying here, watching all my heroes and friends disappear one by one, it seemed people disappearing from your life and watching people leave your life is just another part of getting older.

You start out thinking of people as forever, but they just aren't.

I wait for the car to warm so I can go somewhere far away from this gas station and smoke my cigar, because even though I once ate a dog treat thinking there was chocolate in the middle, even I know you can't smoke at a gas station.

A little wired and still crapping blood and my body tired, I have never felt so alone, and feeling that aloneness creeping up as if from the shadows, I know Jeremy will always be dumb and will always be in search of perfect dirt, and will always be beautiful and a light. I know that Jeremy lost his mom and dad and sister, and I know I'm not even close to knowing that kind of loneliness in my life and still I feel lonely. And because I once ate a dog treat because people I love told me there was chocolate in the middle, for the first time, I understand how someone comes to rob a gas station when their only friend in the whole world asks them to.

....

Jake was also the guy who helped me make pinewood derby cars and taught me to shoot pool. One of his best friends was a woman who had cancer and when she passed he was never the same. There was a toxic dump site across the street from my high school and a few blocks from there, a power plant. A lot of people from my neighborhood ended up getting sick.

Jake once told his mother that after his friend passed, he had a dream one night where he saw God and angels at the foot of his bed. And then his mother went out and told everyone. She told the neighbors and then her friends and then she told my mom and then my mom told me and I'm always the last to know.

I wondered what it would do to a person, seeing God at the foot of their bed or losing their best friend at that age.

Jake used to build cars with his hands. This is how I like to think of him. Mending old broken things. Painting them to look not new, but like themselves.

This one time he put me on his shoulders and said, "Wanna see how fast I can run?"

Now I was terrified of being on his shoulders in the first place and of moving fast in general, but before I could say no, he took off running down the street with me on his shoulders. I've never moved that fast in my life. I couldn't see nothing because I had my eyes closed, but I could feel us both becoming the wind.

part two

tour diary: huntington, west virginia

....

This one time in college I went to Huntington, West Virginia, to visit my girlfriend. That night I went to a party and went diving all headfirst on a slip and slide greased with Johnson's baby oil. I was twenty-one and dove many, many times on the greased slip and slide while she was somewhere else, across town, making sure the students she was in charge of had gone to bed. My hair and skin were baby soft at that party and then softer later when we met up beneath the lamplights that still turned on in those days.

She's a ghost now. Not dead, but completely disappeared from my life.

I'd driven in a day early to surprise her. Her friend planned the surprise by getting her to have a picnic beneath a tree in a parking lot and when I got there I said, "Surprise I'm here."

"I'm so surprised you're here," she said. "You weren't supposed to be here until tomorrow."

That ghost I loved snuck out of her teaching duties that afternoon so we could haunt a stranger's home. We were haunting a place before we knew we could haunt. We were smiling then.

YEARS LATER I've returned to Huntington. Like us, Huntington's different now. It's a little more quiet. Something feels missing. Town looks a little beaten up. The trees we picnicked beneath are dead, and I wonder why no one tells you in school that, like humans, there's so many ways for a tree to die.

Challenging the sun, two friends and I drive to Breece D'J Pancake's grave in Milton, which is about a half hour away from Huntington.

Breece D'J Pancake was one of the most famous West Virginia writers. His only book, his *Collected Stories*, was a gift and rite of passage from my professor Natalie Sypolt. I have since handed off copies to various young writers. It's a kind of talisman passed between mentor and mentee writers, between people of Appalachia you love and the people you want to introduce to a certain kind of Appalachia.

Fiction writers I met during grad school in New York spoke of Breece as a cult figure, as if he was a kind of means toward one's credibility or a currency.

But for us, he was always more a gift meant to be shared.

WE WENT to the wrong graveyard first. Then we went to the other one. It took a while to find his grave because it looked like all the other graves. In the middle of the graveyard, Breece was laid beneath a headstone with regal typography spelling out *B R E E C E   D ' J   P A N C A K E*.

We pulled on a handle of cheap tequila that my friend left in his truck for occasions like this. The sun was sinking tired and slow. From their side of the argyle wire fence, from the backyards of the mobile homes kissing the graveyard, barking dogs signaled: *You've come to the right place. You're here for us and our ghosts.*

BREECE'S MOTHER used to write to Breece's professor James Alan McPherson each Christmas, always suspicious of her son's suicide, which had taken place on Palm Sunday 1979. One day my friend drove all day from West Virginia to the University of Iowa to speak to McPherson about Breece.

An administrator wouldn't let him in the building.

"You don't understand," he said. "I need to talk to James Alan McPherson. I need to know about Breece or the thing inside me won't ever get made right."

"No," the administrator said.

AND I wasn't there with my friend but I like to think that it was fall. That there was a copper wind. That the trees were looking at each other as they started turning into the shame of undressed mannequins, which is shameless because inanimate objects don't possess shame, but if they did, it would be the shame of one knowing they were about to be put away in the storage room for winter. There's something that hurts about not being needed anymore. I bet if a mannequin could feel, it'd feel that.

I like to think of my friend going to a bar, because that's what he'd do. I like to think of him sitting down at a bar in Iowa and having a drink at the bar and looking around the bar noticing things. Noticing not one person in Iowa looked or sounded like him.

These are not my people, he would have thought.

I like to think of him so far away from home in this bar in Iowa that he said *Fuck it* and went back to the writing program building. He walked up to the porch of the writing program and waited. He waited on the porch and waited as more leaves fell, covering the shame of the brittle teeth of the dying and already dead grass, grass that any scientist can tell you does feel. And I imagine shame is a specific feeling grass feels. He waited for McPherson. This until the time when, as all apparitions do, the apparition turned human and he asked the human figure on the porch, "Can you tell me about Breece?"

"You must be from West Virginia," McPherson said.

McPherson must have been on his way either to or from a class (I always get that part of the story wrong). They talked for hours in white rocking chairs on that porch as fall inched its way toward winter. They talked of Breece, of my friend being a young writer, of death and the letters Breece's mother wrote McPherson. They talked on how we talk and write about our dead. How we learn to.

....

As you get older you come to realize you're from where you decide. You're from the community you invest yourself in. Only that's not good enough for some people. Other people don't care, because they're from nowhere, just like us. My name, I hear it most clearly in the hills and rivers and creek beds of West Virginia and when I meet strangers with "West Virginia" on their shirt and tattooed to their chest, talking like West Virginians talk, using ten words when two will do. I hear my name every time it rains and especially when the sky turns over, turns angry, just before it comes down and I can hear it as if it's my grandma saying, "Keegan, it's about to pour the rain," and I hear my name in the smell of the dirt and rocks and after-rain of that place. For better or worse, I made a name for myself in New York City. I was given my name in California. I was born Matthew. Matthew Keegan Rice was my original name. Now I'm Keegan. I was born a Rice and now I'm a Lester. In some ways we're all immigrants navigating—of course, except for those of us who are not. Those of us who are not immigrants or itinerant are those of us who've never been conflicted about the self. Have never heard the whispering from another land, *Come home*. Never had to parse between the double meaning of a word or an image or custom or culture. Never had someone want to talk to you about the white trash they saw on the television last night, and you wonder what part of you comes undone from your costume when they speak. You wonder when they say *white trash* do they mean my *grandma, my cousin, Dad, my friend, my goddaughter*? In the place I grew up, there was no glimpse of West Virginia. There was no place to eat the food that my father was raised on. There was no one who spoke like my grandma or grandpa or believed in magic or the improbable. There were no trains whistling at night and no woods that whispered their secrets.

....

My friends and I noticed everyone here is dying these days, so we left the graveyard and drove back to Huntington and drank while everything turned quiet. It wasn't scenic quiet but scary quiet.

The trains we love for their whistles and whines, tearing night into pieces, which had been our spaceships carrying hope from here to foreign lands and back again, are quiet now. The trains are scary because quiet we know their boxcars could be holding anything.

The streets we used to run drunk and fearless in from party to party are another dead thing now too. The streets are scary because in the dead of their dead street arms, we know the streets are capable of holding anything.

WE WALK to a local place. Have to be buzzed in to enter. Cash only. Coal miners and us pretending to be tough, and men with giant knives strapped to their belts who may actually be tough. But we'll never know. Maybe like looking at a pitbull, our brains are doing the work to trick our eyes and nothing is what we think it is.

I've not yet been killed by a pitbull or even harmed. The most dangerous thing I've ever done is drink the water in West Virginia most of my life and no one talks shit on water universally.

Maybe everything is just itself.

The tree trunk–armed coal miners smoking cigarettes in the bar are still alive. They aren't scary because we've seen so much death that what little that remains alive isn't frightening anymore.

We drink and talk home. Everyone wants to write about West Virginia, but in a way that hasn't been done, which has been done and so we're all stuck.

A police or fire truck or ambulance is the thing replacing

our whining trains in the night. Another fire truck passes us. Every time a siren goes off, someone has overdosed and there are two more people left behind, wondering why in the hell it is that we even try to grow flowers in the Teays Valley when the soil is so bad, and the water is bad and our hearts are good, but too heavy for dropping seeds.

We walk to where we will sleep tonight.

"Don't take that street," a stranger says.

"I got my bike stolen there," a friend says.

"Is anything left open?" I say, hungry.

We eat pizza. We want to write about people. We want to urge you to love this place we love.

How long can we continue loving everything in a place?

THE PEOPLE are good, the land good, the coal companies bad, veterans good, miners good, the politics bad, the water bad, my friends good. Strangers, good. We know how it works.

We know whatever creeps from a mountain's vein, no matter how beautiful a mountain, no matter its need for our saving, if it gets into the water, the water will kill us no matter what one does for the mountain or to the water.

If we continue walking like this, who will visit our graves someday? I wonder. *Who will be left?*

This is what it is to be in love with a place full of ghosts. Well-meaning ghosts.

It's most often what we don't recognize about our ghosts, by which I mean what traits we share with our ghosts, that makes them appear so terrifying.

peaches

....

You never know where you're gonna meet your best friends. I met two of my best friends exactly where most people meet their best friends. I met them at the Humane Society.

This particular Humane Society was in Mishawaka, Indiana, which is a border town of South Bend, Indiana, home to the University of Notre Dame, an Urban Outfitters, and me for a short period of time in 2012.

THE DAY after I met my new best friends, neither of them being the dog I'd eventually go home with, we ate some Thai food, talked about Bon Iver, and had an absolutely terrible rock band practice in my basement that would flood a ton. The basement flooded partly on account that it was haunted by a man who hung himself there a few months before my fiancée and I rented it, and partly because our garbage disposal wasn't very good and the water track backed up into our basement, which is coincidentally where the ghost liked to hang out. Our landlord told us of neither of these issues before renting us the house.

My fiancée and I were getting a dog for the reason everyone in a relationship gets a dog: our relationship was falling apart. We were once given a giant beautiful bulldog that we named Peaches.

"Don't you want to call him something manlier?" the previous owner of the dog said.

"No we like Peaches just fine," we said.

In those days, she and I said everything together at the same time and held hands and named a bulldog Peaches.

OF COURSE I didn't know nothing then about raising dogs or crating dogs or really anything about dogs, and our dog Peaches scared everyone in the neighborhood because he was a bulldog and we would say, *No, don't worry he's just huge and sweet and gets excited sometimes.* But people would scream when he'd run at them, especially when we let him off of his leash at the park. He had bad separation anxiety and I'd have to yell at the people, "Stop running. It only makes him want to be with you more."

Pretty soon we had to stop going to the park.

Peaches was a very sweet dog but had some anxiety. He used to get real bad. A couple times I left him alone in the backyard while I went to work. At the time the only work I could find as a hipster with a graduate degree was at Urban Outfitters.

Urban Outfitters reminded me nothing of New York, which is good because I probably would have missed New York if it bore any resemblance. It was more like working in a high school with a really boring DJ, where everyone tries their hardest to pretend that there isn't better stuff at the thrift store down the street. I had trouble working there because I knew there was better stuff at the thrift store down the street, and also I could never get enough hours and working there just reminded me constantly that I was in South Bend, not New York City.

One day I came home from work and there was a hole in the backyard deep enough that I could step down into it. It would probably have been a pretty good place to hide if at

the time I'd been playing hide and seek. Unfortunately, I had
no one to play hide and seek with because my fiancée was in
medical school and all of our lawn chairs and backyard furniture were torn up and pulled into that hole in the ground and
I was like, *Peaches, I just can't leave you by yourself can I?*
And Peaches looked up at me with his big ole dumb bulldog
eyes that terrified all the children in the neighborhood and
I kissed him on the head, because that's what you do when
your child has done something mildly troublesome but also
magnificent at the same time.

We got Peaches because my fiancée wanted a bulldog.
While I was in graduate school in New York and she was in
med school in Indiana, the thing that made her happiest was
sending me photos of bulldogs flipped upside down with their
gums and faces all loose and all over the place and I learned
the hard way that this should not be the only criterion for
buying a dog. I also learned that people in med school should
not have dogs and people who are twenty-four who do not
know how to take care of dogs, who work at Urban Outfitters part time, also should not have dogs.

Peaches loved eating my fiancée's shoes and purses and
sometimes she would cry a ton back then. Sometimes because of Peaches eating her shoes and purses and sometimes
because of me. And one day we were visiting her family out
in Kentucky and Peaches just ran all over the farm happy as
can be and my fiancée's brother was like, *I love Peaches*, and
I was like, *me too*.

"I THINK we should give Peaches to my brother," my fiancée
said a few weeks later. And I didn't want to, but I agreed
because I felt bad about having to put him in a crate, because
nothing as beautiful as Peaches should ever be put in a cage.
And that night it was storming and my fiancée and I were not
doing so good and Peaches and I sat out on our front stoop
with the overhang above us in front of our little A-frame

house on Sorrin Avenue in South Bend, Indiana. We just sat together a while, all sad as can be for different reasons. I didn't even need to put a leash on him because I knew he wasn't gonna run anywhere because he had separation anxiety and because he was too scared to run, and I knew what that felt like, so we just sat. We sat together and I petted him while we listened to the rain and when I'd see lightning in the sky I'd grab Peaches and pull him close to me, and pull him real tight so he wouldn't get scared when the thunder came yelling and I'd say, "Don't worry, Peaches" as if it was a prayer for both of us.

I think he liked me, but it's hard to tell.

I've no idea where he is now.

....

I met two of my best friends the day my fiancée thought it would be a good idea to get another dog after the Peaches fiasco, even though our relationship barely survived Peaches. Our relationship at that point was not good. But she said I had to decide between a dog or a baby and so I decided a dog was the way to go.

I'd seen it all play out before, but who was I to say anything? I was then a twenty-four-year-old hipster with a graduate degree trying to make a go of it in South Bend, Indiana, working at a mattress and furniture layaway shop. She was the one who was gonna be a doctor. I just figured she knew what she was doing.

And I still didn't know how to take care of a dog. What I did learn was that when you are in medical school you have no time for anyone, not even yourself, but especially not for me or a dog, no matter how cute it looked when flipped upside down with the wind blowing through its jowls.

My friends, on the other hand, were there to adopt a cat, which they still have. That cat is named Coco. My friends are an example of a good relationship.

. . . .

I used to travel between my grad school in New York City and my fiancée's grad school in South Bend, Indiana. One day the journey simply became the trip between New York City and the house my fiancée and I shared.

There was a summer afternoon in Chicago when she and I sat on the ledge of her friend's apartment banister and barbecued. It was the first day that felt like summer because South Bend is so far north that the sun had not quite made its way up there yet. And that day in Chicago the sun had not quite set and it was still warm and we could feel the warmth on our faces and skin, and there were families and hipsters and hipster families with children on dog leashes and young business people walking beneath us on the sidewalks.

There's a Sea Wolf song that I love because it has a lyric in it that goes, *And now I'm lying in the van, Chicago in the springtime, and the rain outside was falling sounds just like popcorn*, and it makes me think of West Virginia, and I thought that day, barbecuing in Chicago there might be another place in the world I could live someday where I would find West Virginia in it and I thought maybe Chicago.

. . . .

One of my last memories in our house on Sorrin Avenue is hearing a dog barking down the street. It was almost Thanksgiving. The streetlights would have been about ready to turn on and I could feel the ocean between her and me.

She was so small in my hands that day and we tried turning ourselves into something else, into what our bodies and minds and hearts had been months before, when we were the small people looking down upon all the other small people below us in Chicago, but try as we did, we couldn't turn into those people.

I remember a banging of kitchen cabinets because her mother was looking for something in our kitchen that she could use to make a stiff drink. Earlier that day I was at my friend's house, whom I met at the Humane Society of Mishawaka, playing NCAA 2011. I was crying because my fiancée and I broke up that morning. Her mother broke off our relationship and then I went to work and cried in front of my boss and his wife and their children.

"I think I'm moving back home," I said.

"Well, before you go, could you move the couches and mattresses out to the front?" my boss said.

While I was crying all over South Bend, my fiancée told her mom, "Maybe I don't want to break up with him."

"Just take him into the bedroom when he gets home and everything will be fine again," she told her daughter.

But we could no longer be the people we were supposed to be, try as we did, and I think we both knew it.

I turned quiet after that.

....

When my fiancée and I were all over, I drove west to St. Louis and saw my friend from high school, Francis Dinh. With him I spoke my first words in weeks. Francis was in a one-year MA premed program and did not seem too excited about it. Francis said, *I hate it here* and *I'm sorry for your break up* and *people are so racist here that even the homeless people won't ask me for money because they think I can't speak English* and *what are you going to do next?*

And I didn't know what I'd do, so I drove to Oklahoma and then Texas and got tired one night in the pitch black of New Mexico. My car pulled me over and I stayed at a creepy motel with no internet and a television with three channels and a Bible in each drawer of the two nightstands cornering a bed with dirty motel sheets. I slept and slept and slept for the first time in a long time. I woke up and I looked all around me and I started singing. I started singing and singing loud as I could and I looked at all of what I couldn't see in the black from the night before and there were mountains of dirt and there was clay of all kinds of colors and it was so beautiful like a child's finger painting. It was just color smeared everywhere. It was like a child took some pastel to the world's walls and didn't care about consequences and everything was smudged with color and so was I. My car was the gravity that pulled me back on to the highway and I continued singing as I drove west and west and more west until I got to a beach. I got out of my car and took my shoes off and placed them on the car seat real quiet as if I might be disturbing someone. It was dark again and I didn't feel much like singing anymore because I'd been singing for some hours then, and then I sat on the beach and wept.

"How the fuck did I get back here?" I yelled.

But the ocean was kind and said nothing.

a year later, in philly

....

Francis was looking at me the way he sometimes looks at me like *you're a crazy person*, which made me wonder if people realize when they look at you like *you're a crazy person* that you know what the expression on their face means. I knew what the expression meant. I knew why his head was tilted at a forty-five-degree angle.

He's looked at me many times this way over the years of our friendship. He looked at me like this in the halls of our high school, and on the top of the Empire State Building on a trip we took to New York City with our Model UN class, when I explained that we should walk to a bar called Mc-Sorley's because my dad suggested it, even though we were only fifteen, and he gave me that look sometimes in the garage where we practiced in our rock band that we convinced his parents was for a scholarship opportunity. Otherwise, all rock-and-roll activities would have been off limits. He looked at me like that the time I said, *You should try to get a tennis scholarship at West Virginia University, 'cause they suck at tennis. How hard could it be to get a tennis scholarship there?* but what I meant was that I just wanted my friend to come to college with me. And he looks at me like that every time I say *Malcolm Gladwell is terrible. Compelling storyteller, but not someone to be believed.*

THE SNOW was pouring in blankets that night.

The entire city of Philadelphia was beneath a blanket of white, howling wind and lightning. Even though we weren't near a television, I knew that at that moment in some television station a poorly dressed weatherman was jumping around a set screaming *Thundersnow* as if it was his Super Bowl.

But for us, maybe because it was too cold for the required breath, it was quiet. We were quiet. It was not our Super Bowl.

I remember Francis stayed quiet. I remember there were lampposts raining yellow beams of twilight on the cars and sidewalks and that bicycle limbs were poking out of the mountains of snow on the sidewalk and that it was beautiful and silent except for our footsteps.

"Tell me again, the story about your uncle when we get back, for the sound check," I said, mostly to break our silence.

Francis nodded.

WE CONTINUED saying nothing as we waited for the crosswalk man to turn green. We say nothing as we cross through the white, icy, untreated roads. We say nothing as we carry our Korean barbecue back to his Temple dorm, which stood out like a strange cousin to all the buildings of Chinatown it edged.

In early December 2012, the neighborhood had all the markings of perhaps having once been a tough neighborhood. The bricks, giving the city a kind of southern quaintness, were covered in elaborate tags, and some of those tags were crossed out by other even more elaborate and loopy graffiti. Scatters of homeless men huddled the best they could under a bridge. They sat on top of stacks of the Philadelphia *Daily News*, which no one was gonna read anyway. A couple of men huddled around a trashcan fire.

This was the kind of night where no one was out that would have been out to stop them from having a trashcan fire. When I see a small fire, I automatically think *samores*, which would not have been the appropriate thing to think at the time, but I'm certain at the time I was likely thinking *samores*.

That night, these men were the kings of the overhang. The overhang is not what the structure was actually called, of course, but "bridge" would make these men sound like trolls and they weren't trolls; they were the kings of this snowy city.

The overhang sat catty-corner to a building Francis described as a kind of mall or deli or mess hall or food court.

"It's a tourist destination, and I get my cheese and meats and clementines there too," he said. Later I found out it's called the Reading Terminal Market. It was closed. Everything was closed.

That night the only thing open was the snow, wind, and homeless people trying to stay out of the snow and wind. We passed rows of closed shops, newly minted coffee houses, bookstores, and bars all with their metal rolling gate jaws shut, protecting precious windows and glass doors and newly installed facades.

It was as if we were seeing the end of one civilization and the beginning of another.

. . . .

In his apartment I tried to look everywhere but directly at Francis as we started interviewing because I didn't want him to be nervous.

I looked at his fridge, covered in Korean barbecue menus, their shiny gloss brandishing K-pop stars in all their K-poppy perfection. I shifted glances to the window and the outside world, which was frigid and white, moisture drooling all over the window. I looked at the coffee table separating us. I looked at his fixie bike hanging on the wall like a trophy behind him and silently judged him. I looked back at his sink full of dishes and continued to judge him silently. The faucet *drip, drip, dripped* to keep the pipes from freezing.

I HAD been going up and down the East Coast gathering interviews for a podcast I was working on and the snowstorm caused all buses between Boston and New York City, including mine, to be suspended. The word that was used was *grounded*, which I found peculiar, as all buses are grounded. I was supposed to be a little outside of Boston that day to interview a photographer who had once been my teacher. There was no telling when I'd make it up there with so much snow now, and I was still living in California then, and with nowhere else to go I bought a bus ticket and headed south to Philadelphia.

A while back I emailed Francis:

Hey Franny, I'm working on a podcast. I need interviews. Can I interview you about your time as an ESL student and how your life turned out after?

He shot me an email back: *Sure. Come any time you want.*

And so here I was, like an idiot, coming any time I wanted, which happened to be during a massive snowstorm that shut down the entire Northeast.

FRANCIS IS studying to become a podiatrist. He's living in a suspended time that one finds themselves in when in grad school. He considers often and out loud the non-profits he wants to work for/create. He wants to perform surgeries in Vietnam on people with a birth defect called clubbed foot. "It would enable those affected to walk again, and by being able to walk, a vastly more productive and more fulfilling life," he says. That's what he talks about when he talks. *Purpose* and *Potential* and Malcolm Gladwell. In grad school, life is full of purpose, potential, fear, self-doubt, and YouTube, which I knew would make Francis a perfect candidate for a podcast interview.

We'd just finished listening to some of the raw, unmixed interview I'd taken with Elaine Sheldon a few days earlier. She was talking about a documentary she was working on, about southern West Virginia and the population decrease happening there and essentially modern-day brain drain in West Virginia, the economics of large swaths of population shifting location, and the crumbling infrastructure left in its wake.

Bleak.

When she said the word *bleak,* her voice dropped into a thick southern West Virginian accent. West Virginian accents are crazy, but not for the reason you think. Even though West Virginia is a small state, it touches five other states and the accents vary widely depending on the region you find yourself in. Elaine is from Logan, West Virginia, which just about touches eastern Kentucky, and just about touches Virginia, and is deep in coal country, so she sounds a mixture of those places when she says *bleak*.

"All the news agencies," she said, "that came to talk to me about my documentary, all printed stories with the same word in it: *bleak*." She said they all said, "McDowell County's future is *bleak*. And it's so infuriating to hear that that was the defining word for southern West Virginia, because if everyone in southern West Virginia thought their future was bleak, I'm sure they wouldn't stay there."

And she's right.

"Oh MY GOD, she's sooooo articulate," Francis said.

"Yeah. Elaine's pretty great," I said. This was before any of us knew Elaine was gonna win a Peabody for her documentary.

AS ANYONE with ties to West Virginia does when hearing someone say *I'm surprised by how articulate a West Virginian sounds*, I took offense, swiftly. The way Francis sounded when he said *sooooo articulate* made it seem that he did not think people from West Virginia could be articulate.

"Uh, do you think anyone will even want to listen to me? I'm no expert like her," he says.

AND THEN I realize I missed something, like the fear in his eyes or his hands fidgeting or that he got all sweaty when he heard Elaine quoting famous artists and calling those famous artists friends and talking about insular cultures and mono cultures and low-hanging fruit, that she wasn't paraphrasing cherry-picked sources that would confirm a long-standing hypothesis she held. She was doing something more. She was telling a story, from her own experience.

And his tells were all there and I missed all my friend's tells, which makes me a terrible friend. I should have been able to read him better as I've known him for about a decade. But then moments like this make me think, *Do we really know anyone or do we only know people as the placeholders we keep in our lives to help us translate events and places and other people and the context of ourselves to ourselves?*

Francis was not surprised that someone from West Virginia could be articulate but was made insecure by an articulate person, which gave him trepidation to tell his own story.

This perhaps stemming from being a child in the ESL program or maybe perhaps from just being human.

As I start making these connections I think: *This is gonna be a really great podcast interview!*

"Franny," I said, "I think we're all capable of telling stories that make us sound brilliant, but brilliant is not what you need to shoot for. We appear to others as knowing usually when we aren't trying to appear that way but instead are telling the stories that move us or stories we've lived or the stories that are necessary. Our stories are all we have and anyone telling their story will sound like an expert."

AND I think I believe that too.

The photography professor said that once in our class. He's damn good at soundbites, which is why he was my first choice for my podcast interview.

AND SO that's what I told Francis that night so he'd let me interview him for the project I was working on. Not the part where my professor was my first choice, but the other thing. The stories thing. Then Francis told me the story about his family leaving Vietnam.

. . . .

"Vietnam was not a good place to be during the war," Francis starts.

"I bet," I said, fiddling with my microphone, probably thinking *I hope I'm capturing his voice warmly*, because I was listening to too much *This American Life* at the time and that was a phrase I heard a bunch.

"My uncle was the youngest of all the males on my mom's side," he said. "When he was eight, him and his three brothers, they left on a small boat. My grandpa prepared food for them and gave them some money and not much else and then let them go because the country was in such turmoil. And they considered themselves lucky because they had found a way out. A maybe."

Francis looked past me as he spoke. His voice turning more deliberate, more fluid in his cadence. His eyes moved somewhere else, to the place we go when we go conjuring. He went to the place in our bodies where we go when telling a story we've told many times. He went to the well in our bodies where these stories are kept.

"So they're on this small boat, and uh, they leave for God knows where just to leave the country and are in the middle of the ocean, and their boat breaks down and they are stuck at sea with no hope. The captain of the boat went beneath the deck, to the others, and said, 'This is the time to pray. If you are Buddhist pray to Buddha. If you're Catholic, pray to Jesus or God.' Right then, my eight-year-old uncle made a deal with God. He said, 'God if you get me out of this, I'll serve you the rest of my life.' "

NOW FRANCIS is talking faster. His words rush like tributaries from a delta into a large body of water. He quotes the martial artist and actor and philosopher Bruce Lee about water and its movement and how water is all the things in a stream because water is malleable. It shapes the rocks and is shaped by the rocks and the fish are water and before my eyes, Francis is turning to water too. He is turning into everything that rushes forward in a stream.

"And my eight-year-old uncle starts praying. He prays and prays and prays and lo and behold, a day later, a large fishing ship came out of nowhere and saved him and took them to Japan, but that's not where the story ends," he says.

The wind outside his dorm was screaming like a beehive between the buildings. The snow piled up in the city. The city, a panache of white and lamplit street stays indifferent toward our existence as it was indifferent toward all the people who lived here before us and all the people living here now and all the people who will one day live here.

"But, of course he forgot about his promise to God," Francis says, "because he was eight. But then in college he had a dream, and God told him to become a priest in the dream. And so he did."

on writing a book

....

A year later I left that beach in California and I moved back to West Virginia for a summer to write a book. After writing every day and drinking every night, summer stopped being summer and what comes after started shaking the leaves from the trees and I started running out of money.

There are people who adore me. People who call me friend and people who look up to me and ask me for advice and guidance. There are people who enjoy spending time with me and care about me deeply. I came to the realization one day that none of these people have ever drunk with me, at least never on more than one occasion. I thought, *This might be turning into a problem*, which is what people think when something has been a problem for a long time. So I quit drinking.

A few days after I quit drinking, my grandpa's best friend died. It was the first time I'd been to a funeral for someone I was close with. It was different from altar-serving. It was different from Shane Rooney. I knew this person my whole life. I knew he was the last remaining friend my grandpa had.

The day after the funeral, my grandma suffered a massive stroke and lost much of her ability to recall words and staple them to her ideas. She'd lost much of her ability to talk.

And as my brain chemicals began to rewire from all the not drinking, all I could see was the hurt in the world I'd caused.

That was a period of time when my grandma and I re-learned language together.

I wrote a book of poems about it that no one wants to publish. I took care of my grandma. I grieved the breakup with my fiancée properly, for the first time. I began wondering if this was what growing up is supposed to feel like: realizing it's possible to love a person very much, admitting it, and realizing you still shouldn't be together. Realizing that just because a relationship ends, you don't ever stop loving a person. We didn't know then that she was dying and I was dying and everything around us was dying too, and we did not understand that our bodies and minds and hearts were betraying each other to survive. For the first time I could see what I'd done to ruin the relationship. Being able to see all of it clearly is what growing up must be, I think.

I also missed Peaches. I wrote poems for Peaches and all the people lost and wandering, who are trying to figure out how to move forward in their lives.

The one thing I know for certain is I'd be dead right now if it hadn't been for my grandma needing me.

political poem

....

In Morgantown that year, I taught writing workshops to four women who were all older, wiser, more accomplished, and far more beautiful than me. They were lawyers and political activists and doctors and I was just me.

Sometimes they would give me rides to places and sometimes they would cook large meals for the class and wrap up leftovers for me, so I'd have something to eat during the week. During that time, one of my students wrote this beautiful poem.

We all sat around a gigantic kitchen table about to go over it, looking at each other, some of us closer to each other's faces than others, and I noticed my other students making the *this poem may be a little too political* face as her forehead kissed the table.

And so what if "fuck fracking" appears multiple times in this twelve-line poem, I think, but I don't dare say it aloud.

"We need poems in the world that will say what we can't," I say to my class.

Part of being a teacher is sometimes saying abstract things with the right words and the correct amount of profound. I don't leave it at that either. Almost in tears I think of the Elk River being contaminated for months now and no media outside the state covering it after a chemical plant leaked chemicals into the drinking water. I think of the two hundred thousand people in that part of West Virginia who can't drink clean water, or shower, or even think of watering their lawns, and the spill was months ago, and people still say the water comes out of the faucet smelling like licorice. People keep saying, "Don't drink the water if you're pregnant," and I wonder how we all aren't pregnant sometimes with ideas.

"More people need to be writing 'fuck fracking,' " I say. And my student lifts her head up from her crossed arms on the kitchen table. And I know she knows I mean it.

I WENT to work today. One of my best work friends, who is more like my mother, is all smiles for the first time in a while, for the first time since her husband broke his foot, which because of that he hasn't been able to work. And it was the first time I've seen her smile like that since she got passed over for a better permanent job in our division, partially because she's a woman and partially because she has a law degree and the division would have had to pay her an almost fair wage.

This one time, the weather dipped down to negative four and I tried taking the PRT to work. The PRT is this buzzing monorail that stops at different points around our town and it always breaks down when it rains or snows. It was the first of its kind and now the only other ones that exist are inside malls or airports where rain and snow can't get to them. And I was so cold that day, but I was managing until I had to get off the PRT and walk the half mile out into the clear white to get to our office building.

After descending three flights of stairs and wobbling across a prairie of icy parking lot, crossing four lanes of traffic and then darting two blocks up the road, I just about made it into the office. I didn't own any gloves then and as I entered the office I took off running, icy tears breaking down my face all half frozen like a Slurpee.

I fell into the building that day, red and broken and blue, clocking in and running to the bathroom, where I turned a knob until hot water spit from the faucet over my fingers, and I just waited there until my fingers were fingers again and could feel and twitch, until they turned back into human flesh.

Walking out of the bathroom and back into our office, my face must have still been puffy red with frozen tears, because my friend said, "Why didn't you call me?"

"I didn't know better," I said.

And ever since then she's made sure I've had a ride to work on the really cold days, but also just when I felt like having a ride. She almost always takes me home after work. She picks me up after dropping her daughters off at school, and they are both super smart and wonderful and sometimes we pick them up if we've stayed a little later than we thought at work before she drops me off. And they both are in their high school's marching band. And they are twins, but different as can be. One always asks me questions about writing and the other always asks me questions about music and a couple times we've even gone to watch the West Virginia University women's basketball team play.

"What are you smiling about? What's got you so excited?" I asked.

"Come here to my desk." She waved me over with her arm in a giant gesture. She always made giant gestures with her arms and eyes and I liked the way she told her stories because they always felt like they were happening in the present and she made me feel like I was in them because of her excited gestures.

"I just found out we've got natural gas under our property. We're gonna let them take it, and I'll still need a job for now, but this is gonna help so much."

And I knew just by looking at the pictures of her husband and their three daughters on her desk that it would help them.

I GET a text that night from a 304 number. Everyone's number in West Virginia starts out 304. I try to play it off real cool.

Hey.

And after some figuring out, I figure out it was just my cousin.

Let's hang out, he texts.

Sure, I text back, not knowing what was going on, because we never hang out. *I don't even have you in my phone,* I think to myself. But we're family and that still means something to me.

WE MEET up at a bar. I've not been drinking for some time now and so I'm sipping on my water, looking around at all the people doing the kinds of things I used to do. Some were trying to talk to women. Some were trying to avoid the men trying to talk them. Some were bouncing around the way you do when a weight's been lifted from your shoulders, when you think the only thing that exists in the whole world is what is right inside here, is right here in front of you, right now, in this tiny bar in this tiny town in this tiny state in this mid-sized country on a medium-sized planet in a tiny galaxy: *this here bar is it.*

"She left me," my cousin says.

"Shit," I say, knowing we'd be here awhile. I get us over to the bar and pull up two of those tall chairs. The kind you see in bars. When I sit, my toes can't even touch the ground, so I let my feet rest on the rung connecting the four legs. I feel like a little kid, like I used to when I'd go sit at bars with my dad, when I was real, real young, waiting on him with a bowl of cherries that the bartender always gifted me and somehow that seems close and far away at the same time. There's so much hope at that age. So much depends on a stranger passing you a bowl of cherries while you wait on your dad at a bar.

A TEACHER once told me faith is like water in a glass. She said you get a set amount of water at the beginning of your life. That never goes away. But as you get older and grow, your glass grows too. And it takes more water to fill that glass, but you only get the water you have. And at some point, we all find something to fill the large emptiness of our glass with, to fill the space that's left over, because none of us possesses enough water.

I look around the bar, and it's all space. All around me is space. I'm watching all the people doin' this dance that I used to do and I feel like I can't wait to leave this bar and go home and sleep, as if when I get there I'll realize I've just learned to dream for the first time.

My cousin drives big rigs. We never really talk, so I don't know much about him or the trucks. I mean I don't even have his number saved in my phone.

"How's work going?" I say to change the subject from his girlfriend leaving him to anything else.

"Just driving the truck," he says.

"How's that?"

"It's alright. The money is okay, but I do some stuff on the side to make enough money to take care of my daughter too."

He pulls a picture of her out of his wallet and shows me. She's got his chubby cheeks and his stormy blue eyes.

I can't imagine helping create a life like that. I wonder for a moment what my child would look like if I ever have one, and as I'm drifting off somewhere else in my wonderment, he says, "I also work with the frackers just outside of town."

He starts getting all teary-eyed when he says this.

And now with all my observing and his talking about his girlfriend leaving him and his baby momma living in Summersville and wanting to get down there more to see his daughter, and needing more money, it's been a couple hours of him drinking and me sipping water and he's all teary-eyed and shit, and I have to pee and he says, "Yeah, I do the drilling part sometimes too. And you know what's the worst part?"

What is worse than the drilling part in fracking? Is there a worse part? I think to myself, but I say, "What?" instead, like an idiot.

"I'm in charge of drilling with this special kind of drill. It's really long and it has the ability to change direction deep beneath the earth. So the people that won't allow us to drill on their land, we go next door and drill deep, deep enough to bypass state law and then we creep beneath their land, while they're sleeping, like fog creeps, and we go deep, deep, deep, below the ground and take their gas from them."

And now he's in full-on blubbering mode.

"It's the worst shit I ever done, to anyone," he says. "I'm stealing, but I need to make the money for my daughter," he says.

"Fuck," I say. And I think it's fucked that we don't have laws to protect ourselves from ourselves, that we don't have laws to protect our drinking water and that all our doctors keep prescribing us OxyContin. I think it's fucked that people can cut down our mountains in the night, while we sleep and dump waste into our rivers. It's because they don't think we're people. And I know they don't. I used to tell people about my grandma when I was young and every time I got to the West Virginia part they would say, "Does she talk like a hillbilly, like white trash?" and I'd say no, she talks proper. And to this day I've never heard a person use language with the elegance and cadence she uses. And she grew up in a coal camp with no running water or electricity.

"Now Ginny, we are gonna need some extra coal if we are gonna keep this schoolhouse warm this week," her teacher would say to her when she was a young girl. So my grandmother would steal coal from her father to keep her schoolhouse warm. My grandmother stole coal from her father so other children could learn to read. She grew up in a coal camp that doesn't exist on a map anymore and if I don't tell her story here, no one will know her bravery. No one will know her heart existed or that any of those people existed. Not even you, whom I tell everything, would have known.

AND SO I think it's fucked that people don't think we're people, that people don't think my grandma is people.

I hope my cousin finds enough money to raise his daughter, and that he finds peace with himself. And I hope my work mother knows I love her the way I love my mother, that her daughters are sisters to me, and I hope she uses that extra money to help her daughters get to whatever place they can dream of. I hope her children look up into the sky at night and see possibility, not a ceiling that's dark and inky, but the stars and the great expanse around them. I hope my student keeps writing the word *fuck* in her poems and whatever she thinks fits after it.

train gravity

....

Then a bunch of people started saying, *I love your poems.*

A bunch of people said, *We want to publish your poems.* A bunch of people said, *Please visit here and read your poems to us.* My grandma said, "I don't know what it is you do, but I think you have to go to . . ." and she couldn't remember the word for New York City, because of her stroke, but just by the way she pointed at the clouds and traced skyscrapers into the air I knew she meant *New York City.*

So I moved back to New York City, for us.

THE WINTER before I moved back to New York City, my friends from the Humane Society of Mishawaka, Indiana, said, "Come hang out with us in Chicago for New Year's."

They moved to Chicago because they'd grown up in a small Midwest town and had succeeded in life. Chicago is the city that people in the Midwest graduate to, but you have to get pretty good test scores to get in. Everyone's real nice there.

And I said, "Alright," and I went to Chicago for New Year's. Before I could set my bags down, they said, "We're getting married next summer," the way my fiancée and I used to say things at the same time. They're one of those couples that is a power unit. If there was an Olympic competition for finishing each other's sentences, they'd win the gold. They've been dating since high school, which I thought was a thing that died out in the movies of the eighties. But no, it still flourishes in the Midwest.

And I said, "I know. I saw it on Facebook," because I saw it on Facebook. "Congrats!"

"Well, we want you to be our officiant," the cutest unit in the history of the world said together.

AND EVEN though I hadn't been to a wedding in fifteen years and didn't know the first thing about weddings and met my friends during a time in my life I often call *the lost years,* I started looking around at their apartment and at their life and it was beautiful. I looked at the television and the Klimt prints above their television, and at the bookshelf with its bookshelf mouth stuffed full of all kinds of books and comics. I looked at their couch and listened to the wind and snow howling outside between the buildings and then there was Coco, the cat they adopted from the Humane Society of Mishawaka. Coco had become a fat cat now. She looked happy and lazy and fat and curled up in a ball of happy-fat-lazy-fur on the couch and I said, "Yeah, of course I will," like an idiot.

....

This morning I'm leaving New York City, hungry and tired and worried I might bump into my ex-fiancée at some point on this trip. It will be the first time I've been back to South Bend since our breakup, at which point I drove west and did not stop driving west until I hit the ocean. The whole drive I was thinking to myself, *SHIT. SHIT. SHIT.*

AFTER I moved to New York, it felt like people changed their mind about the book of poetry that I wrote in West Virginia. People started saying, *I like some of these poems but I can't publish it as a whole.* People were all, *We love your book, but we aren't in love with it.* And I'm like, *Can you describe it in a more constructive denomination than love because I don't even know what love is.*

My book of poetry is all about my failed relationship in South Bend, Indiana, and all the things I didn't know that I didn't know. And all the things I learned when I quit drinking and took care of my grandma. And now I'm on a train back to South Bend, and I don't know the first thing about love, and I'm about to marry my two friends who know everything there is to know about love.

. . . .

Last night I met a girl at a bar who laughed every time I told her I was leaving tomorrow to marry my two friends. She promised we'd eat tacos in Prospect Park when I got back into town. We grabbed a bite to eat on the way to the subway as she stumbled around after the bar, and I walked very soberly, hoping this might lead somewhere.

My roommate had pointed her out as he was stealing my credit card information to buy himself drinks. I sipped on water. He said something dumb and I said, "Oh, you're reading Oscar Wilde," and we spent the rest of the night talking about books and the dumb thing my roommate said. My phone died and so I couldn't get her number, and I gave her mine and she promised to text me.

"Have fun marrying your friends," she screamed at me as she was swallowed by the mouth of the subway.

I never heard from her again.

....

The train launches off out of a tunnel in Chicago. Not like a spaceship. More like a watermelon that needs a bit of a push to get moving. Nothing about this train is fantastic or amazing in any way. And neither am I. This makes me begin to like the abstract idea of this train.

I begin to think the train was conceived to be slow so I would have the maximum amount of time to think about all the times I rode this very train, and all the things that happened after, and about love and death and where we put our hearts when we're done with them.

The train pulls out of a Chicago skyscraper. Then out of the shadows of all the Chicago skyscrapers. Then past the projects and smokestacks of Gary, Indiana, and all the lives in those buildings whose stories I won't ever know. Past the smokestacks puffing clouds into the sky. It's as if these factories were really in the business of making clouds and not in the business of dying.

Then we make our slow movement through rural town after rural town and then the countryside. Each town we pass has identical children running by the train. Watching the children get so close to the train I think, *That's a good way to die.* I think of how many times I've been one of the children running by a train as someone not from here has looked out a window at me.

We pull through the kind of towns where two people could meet in grade school, fall in love, get married, have children, and never leave. Never even think about leaving. The only hints of existence of anything outside of these towns are the trains pulling though and the stars lighting up the sky.

Parts of these towns even have the disguise of home. Mostly the brick and the crumbling porches, the churches and liquor stores and gravel roads and driveways. It's the kids running through alleyways kicking up dirt in their wake that reminds me most of being young in West Virginia and I almost want to get off the train to teach them to chew on honeysuckle.

…………

I've only left West Virginia a couple months ago and I am already utterly homesick, but don't tell anyone.

Within a single month, my roommate has already stolen money from me, used my credit card, demanded I share my bedroom with his cat, and one night I came home and found him rolling around drunk on my bedroom floor with one of my guitars. My guitar amplifier was turned on as loud as it could go, but he didn't know how an electric guitar worked so he wasn't plugged into the amplifier. He was just rolling around on my bedroom floor on his back like he was Chuck Berry or something as the amp sizzled and snickered at him.

He lives in the living room and I have a feeling that I am paying the bulk of his rent too.

"I don't want you or your cat in my room anymore," I said one night when I got up the gumption to say it.

"Fine. You can't use any of my pots or pans or microwave in the kitchen or my shower curtain," he said.

I HADN'T yet considered how important all these items were. He said this knowing he explicitly told me not to bring mine when I moved in, saying there wouldn't be enough room for two sets. He then went to the bathroom and took his shower curtain down from the shower.

I like to call this period of time in my life *The summer of few showers and intense hunger.*

When he'd shower, he'd put up his shower curtain and rod and when he finished he'd take his shower curtain and rod down and hide it, each time he left the bathroom. With nowhere to dry a shower curtain in the apartment, I just gave up.

"Don't even think of bringing any new pots and pans in here either," he said.

I RAN out of money really quick because I couldn't afford to eat out every meal. I lost five pounds and then I lost ten pounds and then fifteen. This morning I weigh about 129 pounds, which is not a good look for me.

People started posting on Instagram, *You ok?* or *You eating 'nuff?* or *You look anorexic* and I didn't want to scare anyone, and I was worried about being a failure after having just moved back to New York and so I said, *YES. YES. NO.*

THIS MORNING at the airport I couldn't even afford the five-dollar Kind bars they were selling. I couldn't rationalize spending five dollars on a Kind bar when I knew that would almost buy me two tacos, which would get me through most of a day, so I just continued being hungry. And now I'm on this train, heading back to the town I once lived in with my ex-fiancée, hungry and smelling like I haven't showered in a week, so I can marry my friends who I met at the Humane Society of Mishawaka.

....

A few shirtless children ride their bikes alongside the train. They have buzzed heads. They ride with us a half mile before peeling off toward some secret part of their town, which exists in every town. The place young boys gather to burn things with magnifying glasses and make up stories about things they thought they overheard their older brothers say. After that, it's the part of the trip I like to call *fields and nothingness*.

A few weeks ago I started reading Scott McClanahan. He's a West Virginia writer. Now he's my favorite living writer. I read his book *Crapalachia*, which is the first time in years I felt someone speaking directly to me in a book. I read it in my new bedroom, feeling hungry and out next to a public pool in Sunset Park, Brooklyn, where I sometimes showered. And I read it on the subway. Sometimes I'd cry in private and public while reading it. Now, I read and reread it when I feel lonely and when I miss my grandma and my friend Courtney and my friend Lisa and when I miss their kids and my cousins and the shit river smell in Morgantown. The book reads like home and I'm rereading it now too, because I read it sometimes when I'm scared, sometimes when I forget that people love me or that I have friends.

HOW THE hell am I supposed to go marry my two friends that I met at the Humane Society in the town where I made bad decision after bad decision by saying nothing at all?

Out the window, more of the same flat field and sun beaming and more flatness and more children running with the train. Each stop a small, small town with the same raised wooden platform looking like the last small, small town.

The people on the train all look the same too. And it gives me the creeps.

A woman sitting a few rows ahead of me begins fanning

herself. She has four giant pink metallic balloons that read "Happy Fiftieth," that bounce around with the rhythm of her hand and with the same rhythm the thought that *Today I'm not going back to our house* bounces around in my head. I'm on a train to the town where I once lived with my ex-fiancée to marry my two friends. And it's no one's fault but the Humane Society of Mishawaka.

SOMEONE'S GRANDMOTHER is reading a *Cosmo* article out loud on the train to her grandchildren. It's all about eating healthy.

"'The trick to glowing skin is kale and ginger,' Keira Knightley says. 'Also, eat lots of bananas.' See? Keira eats her fruit and veggies. If you eat your fruit and veggies you can grow up to become a movie star too," she says to a small boy and a slightly older girl, who are exchanging blows with plastic light sabers.

"Who's Keira Knightley?" the little boy says.

"Elizabeth Swann," the grandmother says.

"Oh, yeah, I want to be pretty like that," he says.

"Eww, you don't want to be pretty," the little girl says.

"You mean you think Kiera is pretty and you want to be handsome so you can marry her, right, Ben?" the grandmother says.

"Yeah, I guess," Ben says, then swings his light saber, connecting with his sister's chin.

"What the *HELL*, Ben."

"Language. Language," the grandmother says. "And, quiet down. Your mother is on the phone doing important nurse stuff. Your mother is pretty special, you know. Super smart. She eats all of her veggies and fruit too. Not everyone can be a nurse."

The grandma looks across the aisle at me when she says this.

"I bet he's not a nurse."

"Nope," I say. I smile.

She thought I couldn't hear her because I'm wearing headphones, but I've been eavesdropping for the last couple towns. It's sweet the way she's talking about her daughter.

There's a couple in their late teens sleeping on each other a few rows ahead of me. There's no better way to travel than with someone you're infatuated with. In front of them, stoic commuters in their uniforms: three-piece suits and a briefcase a piece, Bose headphones connecting them into their iPhones and iPods, remotely, ensuring they keep their distance from the rest of us.

People begin to remove extra articles of clothing as we storm through the Indiana countryside. The heat has escalated from a simmer to a choke and it's the kind of heat that has teeth. Outside the fields are calm and separated into rectangles of color. The summer sky above is blue and constant. A teacher once told me, "One cannot understand a Rothko merely by looking at a reproduction of a given field or painting. One needs to understand it by looking at the brushstrokes. By smelling it. By discerning the thickness and faintness of residual paint according to those strokes. That's where the complexity stems from, not the colors themselves. You miss out on a lot with books and postcards and posters," she said.

Looking out the window, I believe her. And it's because of that, at this very moment I know out in that color at least two people are falling in love. Someone is having their first kiss. People are orgasming. Someone is sharing a lunch and drinking whiskey from a flask out in those colors. Someone else is dying or dead or has been dead for quite some time. Someone's child is being tasked with pulling a sheet over their parent. With closing their eyes for the last time.

All I could see was a fantastic blur of color and space, but I am old enough now to know to leave certain things up to faith, to know things are living in that color and in those brush strokes outside the window.

I fall asleep thinking about all the things the people in those fields have touched.

....

THUD.

It was not apparent when I woke, where the *thud* came from. Then I saw the woman with her happy birthday balloons lying in the aisle between the two rows of seats. Something flowing from her mouth.

Connecting the sound to the woman on the floor, I looked around for help. A commuter in his three-piece suit walked up from the back of the train. He did not stop when he got to her. He stepped over her and made his way up the aisle and into the next car. I began to wonder if it's because she was Black or if the commuter could not handle the commotion. "Can someone help? Do we have a nurse, or someone that can help?" a voice came from my throat, that did not sound like me but was me.

"What's going on, Grandma?" the boy said.

"Is she dead?" the girl said.

"What's that white stuff coming out of her mouth?" the boy said.

And questions continued on and on like that as children's questions will.

The grandmother repositioned the children to the other side of her, up against the window away from the woman foaming at the mouth, passed out in the aisle way. She positioned the children as far away from the aisle as she could.

"Ashley, Ashley, get off your phone," the grandmother said.

"I'm an RN. Everyone back away," Ashley said.

But there was no one there to back away.

Ashley touched the woman, a little too gingerly and I wondered if it's because the woman was Black.

WHEN I lived in South Bend, the only work I could find after my job at Urban Outfitters was at a furniture layaway shop off a highway. Every day my boss talked about "those stupid

Black people." He'd say, "They are dumb enough to leave a deposit on something they will never be able to afford to pick up." He'd say, "They are the easy money," thinking I would agree with him. He'd talk about the stupid white-trash people too. And I had to go every day because I couldn't find work nowhere else and couldn't get money. *Look at that retard. Can you believe how much money that old lady left? She could have just bought the bed she wanted at a regular store.* And I'd have to move beds and mattresses and couches around until I could hardly stand anymore as he said all this.

For some reason my boss was too cheap to by an iPod shuffle and he didn't like the radio because of the commercials, so he copied six or seven songs to a cassette player and played them on a continuous loop from the loudspeaker every minute of every day I worked there. Two of those songs were by Adele and one was "Sexy and I Know It" and the others were all by Katy Perry.

I like to call this period of my life *Learning about racism and pop music at the layaway mattress store of Mishawaka, Indiana.*

I had to learn to make a face. I had to learn to turn my face into something that would not show how grotesque my insides were any time my boss's voice was in reach of my ears for fear I might lose my job. Part of growing older is learning that when you need money, you have almost no control over anything. Part of growing older is learning that when you need money, money is the hardest thing to come by and people will turn themselves inward to get it. I hated having to learn that this is America, but without having seen it I would not understand it the way I can now.

And this means that there was something wrong with me too.

....

Ashley the nurse is performing CPR and another woman has jumped into the aisle to aid her, and whatever appeared racist or convoluted, and whatever notion of those things existing before in my head were eased as these two women attempt to revive the other woman, in the aisle.

....

"You look like shit," my friend Tyler says.

"Thanks."

"No. I mean you look bad," he says.

I couldn't tell if he meant I looked shocked from what I'd seen on the train or skinny from not eating. But I didn't harp on it.

"It was *really* bad," I say. "She went unconscious twice."

"Twice?"

"A train employee came up at one point and said, 'We're seven minutes from the next stop,' and I guess that was the easiest place to get the EMT on."

I turn my head toward the passenger side window and look at all the things that look different now. The gas station's no longer here. My fiancée is not here to pick me up in the car she named Edie. She named it after her grandmother Edith. We named everything either Edith or Virginia after our grandmothers. When she proposed to me, she said we should get married while our grandmothers were still alive. And I was like, *That's a great idea!*

I look out at the train for the first time since getting into the car.

"I wasn't sure she'd make it. I was sure she'd die right there in that aisle."

"Her fiftieth birthday, man. Jesssssssus," Tyler says.

"I was looking down into her face at one point, before she went unconscious the second time. They'd gotten her to sit up and she was trying to cry, but no tears were coming. Like I could see her trying to force her muscles to cry, and there were no tears. Her tear duct reservoir was all dried up and I've never seen fear like that before. I was offering her my water and she sipped on it before going unconscious again. And the whole cycle repeated itself."

"That's scary," Tyler says, fiddling with the radio.

THE BLUES and reds make their orbits above the ambulance. There are no siren whines and so Tyler and I just sit in the car waiting for the paramedics to blast off so we can leave the parking lot.

This train station looks like all the other train stations across Indiana. Just a small wooden platform.

"It just feels like I was completely powerless. Like I'm useless as a human being. Like, if it ever comes down to it, like a life-or-death situation, and I was the only one around, it would end in death for someone, for sure. I don't even know CPR anymore."

"You could write about it," Tyler jokes.

"I could write about it. I will write about it."

"Like the angel of death or something, just hovering around waiting on people to die, to write it."

"Yeah, exactly. I mean we're all are just waiting around for people to die."

"Well, that's dark."

"Are you ready to get married?"

"Yeah. Are you ready to marry me?"

"I guess."

"You look hungry as shit. Uh, wanna grab some wings?"

"Yeah. I'd love to."

"I was also thinking, since we are so close by, we could go check out the dogs at the Mishawaka Humane Society."

"Man, let's just go get some wings, so Alyssa doesn't kill us," I say.

Driving through South Bend, I remember the kindness and patience of my fiancée's heart. I remember how when we found out from our neighbor that a man hung himself in our basement, we then realized that the ghost was always watching over her. That he'd make the rooms I was in cold and the rooms she was in warm and would slam doors for her when she was mad and would sometimes sing late at night when ghosts think no one can hear them sing. But I was up 'cause I was so afraid for my future. And then I was so afraid of this phantom singing and it made me move even closer to her in our small futon bed. Right then in that bed next to her at night, I did not know of all the places I'd one day get to see and all the strangers I would meet and all the people I would come to love. I did not know then if I'd ever get to smell that shit river smell again or see my grandma alive or if I'd ever write a book worth publishing.

I didn't know anything.

I know more now, but not nearly enough.

I look out the window and Martin's Supermarket is still there with a line in front of the Redbox video dispenser.

"People here still haven't caught on to Netflix," I joke.

"Same old South Bend," Tyler says.

THERE WAS a night where she and I were standing in the grocery store parking lot eating ice cream, sitting in the trunk of our Subaru, looking up at the moon and the moon was so big and hung so low, I thought we could touch it. I thought we could touch anything. So we drove to a nearby park and started swinging from a swing set. We swung and swung and swung higher and higher and jumped, just barely missing the moon each time, by inches.

"Tyler, I don't think we should go to Humane Society tonight."

"Why not?"

"Well, it's a few days before your wedding. What are we going to do if we end up with a dog? Alyssa is going to kill us."

WE WENT to the Humane Society of Mishawaka anyway and we petted a bunch of dogs and played fetch and handed out treats and then we washed our hands. We pulled out of the parking lot and it was dark then. Darkness was all around us and we drifted across town to the wing place and ate some wings and in Tyler and Alyssa's love and in those wings and in the few moments at the wing place with all the televisions yelling about who would win football this fall and who would win football in the coming weeks and in remembering how low the moon once was, that I could nearly touch it here, and even in the damned Humane Society of Mishawaka, I'd finally found West Virginia in something.

part three

tour diary: alabama

....

We didn't know what we were going to see in Alabama until we saw it. I didn't know I was going to be in a gay bar my first time in Tuscaloosa, until I was in a gay bar for a reading called Sacred Grove. Nor did I know everyone would be so beautiful.

In the gay bar I ran into a person whose partner knew me from West Virginia. I thought Nick Saban would be the only West Virginian I might run into in Tuscaloosa. I thought of my father. It's strange to think my father and Nick Saban went to high schools fifteen miles apart around the same time and how different and how much the same their lives turned out and I didn't know I'd think about my father or Nick Saban or Fairmont, West Virginia, while standing in a gay bar in Tuscaloosa, Alabama, but there I was thinking about them.

We had no idea we'd have to change in front of a fraternity. Changing in parking lots had become the norm, though this one wasn't as dark as we sometimes hope parking lots may be in situations like these. We were late leaving Nashville because our new friends in Nashville wanted to show us their home, which is so much what new friends like to do. Four hours later, I was in a different state, in a parking lot, in my boxers, and some well-dressed men with expensive haircuts and blazers and shined shoes howled at what I thought was the moon but was my super white legs lighting up the night, spilling out of the car, in a parking lot in Tuscaloosa, Alabama, just moments before a poetry reading we were late for, featuring brilliant people from Tuscaloosa, Alabama, and Riverside, California, and *us*.

Alabama is more than that too.

A few days later we couldn't stop the car because we were late leaving New Orleans and had to be in Tallahassee that evening, but I wish I could have stopped somewhere on the coastline and sucked on crawfish on top a worn-down pier, beneath an umbrella next to a hand-painted sign with the words *crawdaddies, hush puppies, po'boy, crab claws, baked potato with the fixings*, and *cold beer* and watch the sun set over the tiny fishing boats and bridges, listening to the songs of the black-necked stilts and the oyster catchers and the swooping pelicans, mouths knowing infinite elasticity, a black hole swallowing stars, trying to steal our lunch away. Perhaps, later we'd read the black-bellied plovers' secret messages scribbled with their feet into the shoreline's hard-packed sand before the ocean's fingerling waves brushed away the scribbles. Then after that we'd have to start over again.

And I wouldn't mind a bit having to start over.

The sand dunes in Alabama are like a child of the ocean. From the ocean's womb they evolved over millions of years from waves breaking sediment and tides carrying sand from further out in the ocean to the shore. The dunes absorb the energy created by their relatives, *the storm waves*, minimizing the damage of storm against the beach. It was as if the ocean knew it would one day need a safeguard from itself and from itself made something to protect others from itself. The grasses sprouting are another generation of this family, keeping the sand in place when the wind comes calling names.

But we didn't get to stop on this trip across the state of Alabama because we were late for a reading in Tallahassee.

AND I don't know why it is people have children. Nicole Kidman, in a film I love, says it's because *We realize things are screwed up beyond repair. So we decide to start again.* She says, *You will succeed where I have failed. Because we want someone to get it right this time.*

But because I've not had any children, I'm no expert on the topic. I just know how sand dunes work. And I've no idea about children, the same way I knew nothing about Alabama until in a restaurant in Tuscaloosa, that night after the reading.

"Where y'all from?" the young man waiting on us asked.

"All over," I said.

"What are you doing here?"

"We're writers, on tour."

"Wow, real writers and you came all the way here for us," he said. "I like to write too," he said, and I thought about years ago working at a layaway mattress and furniture shop in Mishawaka, Indiana, that I thought I was dying, and I was dying and couldn't do a thing about dying and could do nothing about the night it started snowing and I was in shorts throwing mattresses into the back of a loading truck. I could see crystals in the snowflakes because the loading deck lights were on as the snow fell all soft and snowy and I slowed for a moment to catch a snowflake on my tongue.

"What the fuck do you think you're doin', Keegan?" my boss said. And he was right. *What the fuck am I doing?* I thought.

"Write, if you love it," I told the boy. I said, "It will take you places you never thought you'd have the chance to go." I told the boy, "I've sold more books at Domino's Pizza takeout shops than bookstores, because the only people that really love poetry are the people living it."

I didn't know that I was going to be in Tuscaloosa, Alabama, the snowy night I was throwing mattresses from the loading dock in Indiana, but I knew my grandma was getting older and I kept saying, *If she dies before I get to see her again, I don't know what I'll do.* I didn't know that I was going to get another chance to go back to West Virginia and write a book and throw paper airplanes with my grandma and watch them climb into the air. I didn't know I'd get to go back and swim in lakes and get too drunk and stop getting drunk and move away again, until I moved back and swam in lakes and got too drunk and stopped getting drunk and moved away. I didn't know then what kindness means to people, until strangers were kind to me and I didn't know what strangers mean to strangers until I left to meet them.

grandma

....

loves getting dressed up all fancy in her tan pantsuits with her blouses that are borderline psychedelic, full of color and geometric shapes, a string of pearls and tennis shoes. She loves drinking pink, pink cosmos, especially if you dress up the rim with sugar, and she loves sugar and candy and vinegar and lemons and vinegar and sea-salt chips and is skinnier than a rail. And more than anything in the whole wide world, maybe even more than me, Grandma loves gambling.

Casinos love her too.

She has Mirage drinking glasses and Trump Plaza jackets and a waffle maker that makes waffles with *Trump* in the center, and she even once gave me a television that a casino just gave her because they were such a fan of her gambling. She gets so much mail from Vegas and Atlantic City, I swear she's got her own personal fan club.

She can be hard-nosed. She taught me sarcasm in the kitchen as the men sat around the dining table in the other room. On the back porch she'd smoke Virginia Slims and say, *Keegan, it's alright, I don't inhale,* and *Don't do this.* And she's outlived just about everyone she knows. She says, *Don't believe anything you hear,* but she always has a hot take, usually about the people in the room. She never shies away from saying it, no matter how uncomfortable it makes them. No matter how many days my uncle whines about it to everyone after.

She's just always telling it how it is.

She used to beat the hell out of me in checkers and gin rummy when I was young, saying, *You'll never learn any other way.* One time she accidentally broke the wristwatch of a student of hers with a ruler because he kept talking during class and she got scared sick over it because the boy was wealthy. The father of the boy came in the next day to confront her. When she tells the story she always tells us, *I thought he was going to kill me. I thought he might shoot me or beat me up. But he just made his son apologize for talking and said, "Thank you for hitting my boy and setting him straight." That boy was a little angel in class after that. I probably should have hit more of my students.* And then she laughs.

She talks of nights in the coal camp she grew up in that were so cold that her mother would leave jello on the windowsill in her room and there would be a layer of frost on the top when she woke. She said her mother was so sweet and would warm up the bed before she and her sister would go to sleep at night. She said that some people are made too sweet for this world.

And hard as she is, and as much as she loves telling it how it is and breaking watches and cursing like a sailor and smacking mouths, she also cries a bunch. She cries whenever I have to leave her or when my dad flies back to the West Coast or when schoolchildren sing. Sometimes she cries when looking at other people's children at church or when town gets dressed up for the holidays, and sometimes she cries when she thinks her children are mad at her for telling it how it is. She's the strongest person I've ever known. Because of that I always understood crying as just a part of strength.

She loves pretty things too. She loves flowers. Even before her stroke she was not much good at keeping these pretty things alive. My aunt brings her a new rhododendron each summer and it always dies. And sometimes when my grandpa is in trouble for saying the wrong thing, because he's always saying the wrong thing, he brings her flowers and they die and sometimes people visiting her bring flowers and they die too and she says, *Shit. Shit. Shit. What did I do this time?*

Before I left West Virginia, I got her a pot of fake flowers.

When I call her, she says, *Keegan, I water them every day.* When I call her, she tells me, *They grow more and more beautiful with each passing day.* When I call her, she tells me, *I can't believe they're still alive.* She says, *I've never been good at keeping anything alive before.*

christmas is a big deal in my family

....

And I know what you're thinking: *SO WHAT? Christmas is/ isn't a big deal in my family.* And I know what else you are thinking: *We love presents and love/hate Jesus too.*

In my family Christmas is a big deal because it's my dad's birthday.

I used to hear stories about how when he was growing up, for Christmas he got to pick out one present and for his birthday he got to choose what he got to eat for dinner, which was usually pancakes. That was it for the year.

So everyone in my family always tries to make it extra special for him. This was true, even when I was young. I never know what to get him, except for this one time in third grade.

MY SCHOOL was selling things in the library all week, the week before Christmas break, and I thought, *Man, I can't afford anything cool.*

I didn't see much of my dad in those days, unless I was about to get spanked or was going to Mass. He left for work before the sun came up and he came home after I went to sleep. The sound of his Astro van's engine turning over is the sound I hear to this day when I think of him.

The only other time we hung out, other than when I was in trouble or going to Mass, was sometimes we'd sit in bars together and listen to live music. And sometimes we'd sit in bars together and watch West Virginia University football games. And it must mean something that the only things I've ever wanted to do were be a West Virginia University football player and sing in bars to strangers.

THAT YEAR I was looking at all the things at the fair in my school that I could buy my dad for Christmas. There were books about Jesus, and there were shirts that were too small and every kind of ashtray conceivable and a couple vases and a rack of belts hanging by their buckle like bats. There was no way I was going to spend my lunch money to add to my dad's belt collection.

Then I saw it. It was perfect. It was in a box, but beneath the cardboard I knew it was shiny and perfect.

Staples. Tons and tons of staples.

I spent all my hot lunch money on staples. Four boxes worth of staples. I thought, *My dad loves to work. He'll love staples.*

In class we wrapped up our presents we'd bought at the fair and I wrapped up my boxes of staples in tissue paper and the wrapping paper my teacher gave us and she said, "Keegan, what a great present. Your dad will love this!"

I must have been swaying side to side or something because she also said, "Keegan, you sure do look hungry. Are you okay?"

And my head was humming because I was pumped so full of adrenaline from finding the perfect gift and Ritalin because my teacher and classmates and parents and little sister found me insufferable and I said, "Nah, I'm great," all shaky like a fiend.

I REMEMBER SLIPPING the box into my dad's stocking that year after everyone went to sleep but before Santa came. We all had stockings. Red stockings with white cotton trim and each one had raised glittery ink with our names. One said

Mom and another said *Dad* and another said *Paige* and another said *Keegan*. And it was just one big ole family of stockings hanging over our fireplace like a family portrait.

The next morning my little sister tore through her presents and I got yelled at because I was always getting yelled at and my dad pulled my present out of his stocking and said, "Oh. What's this?"

"Happy Birthday, Dad," I said knowing I'd found the perfect gift for him.

He opened it up.

"What's this shit?" he said.

"Staples! For work!" I screamed, excited as could be.

He opened the box up, touched the long pack of staples with his expert hand. "This isn't even the right size staples for my stapler."

"Joe," my mother said.

"Uh. Thank you, Keegan, for this great birthday present," my dad said.

AND I'M not sure what happened the rest of that Christmas morning, but I'm sure I got spanked at some point for not being able to sit still long enough. My dad still has those staples sitting on his desk to this day. Partly because they remind him of me, and partly because I couldn't even get staples right.

....

"Grandma's in bad condition. I don't know how much longer she's gonna make it."

So I packed my stuff up and got on a Megabus the next morning, early, and the stars were still out popping and the marquees were still lit and moving and it was just me and a few stray lovers hand in hand.

I bus all the way to New Jersey, all the way through Pennsylvania, all the way to West Virginia, and my grandpa says, "How's New York?" and my uncles and aunts and cousins say: "How's New York? How's New York? How's New York?" And I say, "Great, Great, Great, Great, Great," all believable. But it's not. I even grin all wise like a monk, as if I'm hiding some knowledge about how great everything is.

Grandma didn't say anything.

She'd been coming along okay after her stroke while I had been living in Morgantown but struggled after I left. Really what she needed most was a partner in crime who had some idea of nutrition. Someone to talk shit with, to break rules with. Someone to take her gambling at one of the hot spots in town. Someone who she could trust, who believed she wasn't crazy, who also might tell her, *You need to eat more than potato chips and cosmos.*

And I knew she wasn't crazy. She just really loves drinking

cosmos and gambling and listening to rock and roll. There's nothing crazy about that.

Some days we'd make paper airplanes and throw them from her balcony over Morgantown and watch the air streams lift them up and carry them up, up, up until we couldn't see them any longer.

My dad had moved my grandparents into an apartment above a hotel in town so they wouldn't have to go up and down steps anymore and because their house had become too much to take care of. The only problem was, now there was no place for either of them to escape each other. And all I know about love now is that as people get older they need places to hide from each other or a war will break out.

EVERY FEW days we'd convince my grandpa to drive us to Applebee's so my grandma could get a salad, because she loves salads. Only this salad had the same calorie and sugar content as a birthday cake. And the only thing my Grandma likes more than salads and gambling and rock and roll is sugar and talking shit on people sitting around us in public as if they can't hear us, because she can't hear us.

But they could hear us because she'd talk so loud on account she can't hear worth a shit anymore.

Sometimes I'd get her to go on walks with me and we'd walk down by the river and look at the ducks and geese and she'd say, *It's such a beautiful day in the neighborhood,* as if she was the first person to ever say it and some days I believed she was the first person to ever say it.

There's a mosaic mural down by the river that we'd pass on the way to the bridge that she likes to walk to. We'd pass it again on the way back home and both times she'd stop, study it and say, "This is the most beautiful thing I've ever seen." Each time we walked by it, it was like Christmas morning. It was like the first time she'd ever seen it.

The mosaic is a ceramic tree with fish-shaped leaves. And each leaf is decorated different by some person or organization in town. And it forms this gigantic tree and the metaphor is supposed to mean that we are all equal and different and the sum of us together makes up this beautiful thing. This ceramic tree. This metaphor and literal ceramic mosaic tree.

Some leaves have mirrors, like the people who help you see yourself better, and some have sea glass like the people worn down by life that we find beautiful, whose experience no longer cuts us but is something we keep our eyes peeled for because we want to hold onto their stories. And some leaves are painted wild like the people so badly trying to show you the world they see, which helps dislodge us from the colors we've grown accustomed to. There's Jewish symbols and Christian symbols and African and Asian symbols. And my Grandma may be tough as shit, but she also cries at things she finds beautiful.

Because of my grandmother, I've never been afraid to cry either.

And she cries twice, each walk.

And just like we need all these leaves, we also need these tears too.

EVERY MORNING I wake at four because we all have to be on my grandfather's schedule. I cook breakfast and lunch and dinner and my Grandpa says, "I don't want to eat any of that healthy crap, and I don't think your grandmother does either." When finished cooking, I clean their home and fix everything. I fix the mechanical blinds, their internet, their radio receiver so they can listen to their music out on their balcony and listen to their television through their surround sound, which is mostly just Judge Judy yelling at poor people, and Fox News yelling at people, saying, "The Mexicans are gonna invade this country, the Mexicans are gonna steal our jobs, the Muslims are going to invade this country. The Muslims are going to steal our jobs," over and over in such a way that I don't even know what's real anymore.

Every day I whisper to my grandmother, "Everyone on TV is a liar. Don't get scared."

"I know, Keegan," she half yells, thinking she's whispering.

She can't hear anymore and my grandpa can't hear her yelling because the television is turned up so loud.

"None of those women with blonde." She pauses for a moment trying to find her words. "Their hair can't be real. I think they all wear wigs," she says.

Every day I hug her and say, "I love you, Grandma."

"I know you do," she says.

WE GO on walks and talk every day until she's not afraid to talk to people again. Until she has no trouble with language again.

"I can't believe all the things you can fix," Grandpa says after I get the broken ironing board to collapse one afternoon.

"Anything is possible with the internet," I say.

"I just thought you did fancy stuff," he says.

"What do you mean?"

"All the fancy college New York book crap."

"Oh, I like to fix things too."

FROM 6:00 A.M. until noon the TV screams with Fox News and then Andy Griffith and then Judge Judy and then Judge Brown and then Judge Mathis and then he has happy hour at four and he drifts off into sports as I make dinner.

"I don't know about that crap," he yells when the smoothie blender begins to whine. It's the only way I can think of to get more nutrients and protein into my grandma.

Each day my grandma gets a little better.

"Now, just wait a second, what the hell do you think you're doing, Keegan?" my grandpa says one day after I clean the fridge of spoiled food. "Can you watch her while I go out and pick up some more groceries?"

MY GRANDPA lost his best friend a few days before my grandma suffered her stoke. My grandpa and his best friend did everything together: pinochle, going to church, drinking, talking shit on the entire town, talking football, talking shit on people that attend their church, talking shit on the football team. They did everything together.

They used to sit on the porch in the summertime drinking Jim Beam with a splash of water, back when my grandparents still lived on South High Street, right across the street from a synagogue. In one direction sat a fire station and in the other a graveyard and when I was young they would tell me stories about growing up in Morgantown and being children during World War Two and watching Jerry West play basketball in the old field house and selling apples at the games because none of them had enough money to get in. And then during the winter they'd go get coffee at McDonald's and shoot the shit together, as he described it, with a real smart *eye-ranian guy* and this *eye-talion*. But because one day everyone had died and it was just him and the eye-ranian guy and who knows what that guy would have thought about my grandpa, especially after my grandpa kept calling him eye-ranian all those years, he stopped having people to talk to and a reason to leave the apartment.

My grandma changed dramatically after her stroke. She's the same person, you just had to play word games to understand what she was getting at. But my grandfather is no good at word games or thinking abstractly or joking around or having fun and to him it was as if she had passed too. He felt like he couldn't leave her alone, and it upset my grandma. It drove them both crazy. So he never left the apartment except to buy things from the grocery store, which meant they had more rotten stuff than anyone knew what to do with. He'd go to the store every day and buy stuff they didn't need because he thought it was the only thing he was ever allowed to leave the apartment to do. I wish someone would have told him he had permission to go meet some people and talk shit so he'd feel better.

Sometimes he'd stay out for a couple hours at a time, and I wasn't exactly sure what he was doing, but I hoped he was at McDonald's talking to someone.

I WAS always happy when he went to the store because I knew he needed it, plus it was the only part of the day I wasn't listening to Fox News dialed up loud enough that two people with severe hearing disabilities could hear it. This is when my grandma and I would turn up the rock-and-roll channel on the television and dance in the living room to Buddy Holly and Ritchie Valens and Fats Domino or she'd grab a newspaper and read it or look at the clouds out the window and some days she would say, *Keegan, I can see the faces of my Dad and my brother in those clouds. Keegan, I miss them so much. Keegan, what do you see in those clouds?*

AFTER A little purging of their fridge and preparing meals, and talking to my grandma and making fun of my grandpa with her, and giving her hugs and telling her "I love you, Grandma," every day for a month, she was finally getting better again.

But I, in the words of my grandma, was beginning to look like shit. And she'd tell me. Grandma would say, *Keegan, you look like shit.*

I was tired and worn down with my grandpa's schedule. I'd been back nearly a month and maybe left the apartment two times. I didn't get to see friends or their children. I went to the Blue Moose cafe twice, which is the coffee shop in town that has gigantic tables and perhaps is the best place in town to write and people-watch, and all my friends used to work there and the place has giant windows so people can see you in there and come stop by and say, "Hi, how you been?"

Now that I'm old, a new generation of people at the Blue Moose is making coffee and playing songs that sound like the same songs playing over the sound system as when I went to school, but with different band names.

BY CHRISTMAS my grandma was upright and talking to people and you would never even have known that she was in bad shape a month prior.

You know when my grandma is doing well because she starts telling it like it is. She'll say, "You know, your grandpa walks like Moses. Have you ever seen anything move that slow?" Or "Those college students out there, one is dressed worse than the other. They look like shit. You'd think they just rolled up out of bed and go to class." Or "All those ladies on Fox, they must be wearin' wigs 'cause no one's hair looks like that and they don't say anything at all. I wish Fox would hire women who aren't so dumb." And these were all the things Grandma said at Christmas that year, which was my first Christmas without my mom and dad and my younger sister.

AND SOMETIMES it's hard to see people taking charge in your own house. After a while Grandpa did not want to just control the television but other things too.

"Now, Slick, let me show you how to clean the floors the right way," or "Now I don't want you joking with Grandma like that anymore 'cause she won't listen to me" or "Keegan, no more of that healthy crap."

And then my grandma had some bad days. My grandpa got more mad and my grandma got mad because my grandpa was mad and he made her life difficult, more difficult than I could make it better. And she had some more bad days. And once I'd gotten my grandma healthy enough, my dad said,

"Yeah, let's fly them out to California, and your mom can look after them a while."

The weekend before they left for California we went to Mass because it makes my grandma happy to see her family in church. She can't hear a thing that's going on though, so she likes to talk to me about what everyone in church is wearing and how nice the singers sing and how one of my uncles looks like a mess and how beautiful the singers sing and how nice the family with the two young thirty-something-year-old parents with four kids look and how beautiful the singers sing and how even though she can't hear most of what the priest is saying how she thinks his homily was wonderful and how beautiful the singers sing and then she waves at everyone in the church even at the people who don't know she's waving at them. After all that, my grandpa takes us out to brunch. He says, "Slick, when are you leaving?"

"Two Tuesdays from now I'm gonna catch a bus back to New York."

"But we are leaving Friday. Where do you think you're going to stay?"

"Just in the apartment a couple days and catch up with my friends."

"Who told you, you could stay here while we were gone?"

My grandma shoots him a look but doesn't say anything. And that was the day that Keegan's bedroom, as my grandmother and I knew it, stopped being Keegan's bedroom and became the guest room.

"You're lucky I didn't make you pay rent for the time you stayed here," he says.

....

They got on a plane and flew to California to spend a month in the sunshine with my parents and I sat on my friend's couch in Morgantown and I drank scotch, neat. This was when I started drinking again.

In the pictures I have from that night I look like a late 1960s version of Bob Dylan. This is *skinny tired-looking Bob Dylan* where his manager said, "Bob, if you just add another sixty dates to the tour, you'll be a millionaire," and Bob said, "Whoever said I wanted to be a millionaire? This is going to kill me." Now I realize that Bob looked the way he did not just because he was on speed or because his body was tanking, but because all the people around him who he had depended on his whole life to see him the way he saw himself, no longer saw him as that. He was just a famous person now. He had become a commodity. And people are capable of committing incredible acts of cruelty when they lose sight of another's humanity.

It felt like I'd lost the version of home I'd depended on my whole life to carry me through.

MY BRAIN was beginning to rewire from the stress and I started losing it. Because I was taking care of my grandma, I missed Christmas for the first time ever with my mother and sister and my dad. Taking care of my dad's mother was the only decent birthday gift I've ever been able to give him.

My dad called me before I left West Virginia and said, "Didn't feel much like celebrating this year because it felt lonely and empty without all of us together."

And I thought, *Maybe this is what growing up is.*

For the first time in a long time, I missed my mother and father and sister, and I wanted to go to California and I wanted to drive along the Pacific Coast Highway with my sister and sing songs in our car. I wanted to see our dog and I wanted to sleep. More than anything I wanted to sleep.

....

I took a bus back to New York City. When I came out of the Holland Tunnel, all the buildings surrounding me were mine and the stomach of that city was mine, my home, and I stepped off that bus and right back into the streets and then into another building where I exist as one of the millions of windows my neighbors will encounter in their lifetime.

ernest

....

It's raining.

It's almost always raining when I have to leave my apartment to perform. I have to take three trains to get from my neighborhood in Flatbush, Brooklyn, to the Lower East Side.

It's a strange and beautiful evening. The sun's not quite gone down yet. My neighborhood is filled with families that have lived here for generations. The subway platform is above ground between two buildings, and the rain that's collected in the gutters runs off the overhang at either side of the platform.

On the subway there are families with their children and teenagers with high school athletic equipment partially on, on their way home from practice and folks heading out to their second and third jobs. I'm wearing a sweater and jeans and my comfy slip-on shoes. I've got a backpack with my costume in it.

Like most costumes we wear, mine is merely the more fleshed out version of myself in my mind, that I may or may not be, that I want to be or am becoming.

My neighborhood and I hum underground together awhile, until the DeKalb Avenue stop at which point we crawl out of the ground and into the sky, up and over the Manhattan Bridge.

The millions of blooming lights of New York City are before us. The sun has sunk its head and night has unfurled its arms and for the five or six minutes it takes to get over the bridge, all the wonder and awe of the city is around us. Then we tuck back beneath the ground and I change trains. And then I change trains again and get off the subway, climb a flight of stairs out of the ground and up onto the Lower East Side of Manhattan, right on the border of Chinatown.

At this moment, I still feel like myself. This still feels like New York.

The arches of McDonald's are shining and people are selling trinkets on the sidewalk. No one seems to care about a little rain.

I still feel like myself when I turn the corner and walk about halfway down the block and into the alley, careful to avoid puddles that have gathered in the chewed-up asphalt. I walk a little ways and then turn into another alley and then there's a large industrial-looking staircase leading up to a large man standing on what might have once been a loading dock during the Civil War. We are both tucked into the stomach of the city now. The man doesn't ask for my ID because I'm early. He knows I'm here to perform at the show. He gives me a nod and opens the door.

The room is covered in intricate wood paneling and royal red wallpaper from the 1920s. There are a few taxidermy animals hanging throughout the room. Deer and jackalopes and a giant black bear. It's a large room that has a second floor and a staircase that has the feel of grandeur of the *Titanic*. A band is practicing 1920s standards up on the stage. A tarot reader is setting up her table and a few people are tasting absinthe out of teacups.

It feels like a movie or theater set. The show hasn't started. The suspension of reality that our brains will perform has not quite activated. Right now, it's just a room. We are just people walking an organism that is not quite breathing yet. People are scrambling to get decorations up for show time. I walk up the stairs to the second floor, which is full of tables and couches and lounge chairs and spooky paintings, where people's eyes follow you around the room, and I still feel like myself.

At the back wall I pull the bookcase, which is a secret door, to a room where later we will perform private poetry readings to a paying audience, and further behind there, our dressing room.

I START undressing and put on my costume and other folks are putting on their costumes too. Backstage there are writers changing and burlesque dancers changing and people with jobs in finance and jobs teaching high school changing and we are all changing into our costumes, becoming the selves we are, but too afraid to commit to. We undress and become the people we were meant to be. And everyone is gorgeous.

I love this space. I love the dressing rooms and the show happening behind the show. The energy of an entire team of people coming together to make a show happen. The part of being a writer I love the most is performing. So much of what I do, I do by myself. Here I get to see the looks on the faces of people, who have no idea what to expect. I find out if jokes are landing, if I can suck the breath from someone's chest.

The gossip in the back room is popping about. I love all the sharing of what it is we've done or what has hurt us since the last time we were dressing into our true selves together.

From behind the bookcase I emerge Ernest Pettaway, the soft spoken, sentimental, bourbon-drinking Appalachian itinerant—never quite free from the chains of the place calling him home. The world around me is different too. Full of masquerade masks and sequin dresses and music. Full of people who for a few hours will perform the magic that is the suspension of belief.

This is the place where I learned to become a performer and write for others. If you met me sometime after 2015, this is the person you've probably met. Ernest.

....

A few months before on another rainy night, I read my poems at a bookstore for a reading that was tied to the release of a literary journal. It was put on by folks in the Brooklyn poetry scene, a group of people I do not belong to. The reading itself felt like most readings.

There was a podium, as if the reader were a lecturer and not an artist. The podium is there to separate the writer from the crowd. A line that constantly reminds folks of which side they are on. Much of the work was overly wrought and unnecessarily heavy and hard to follow. I had a teacher who once said, "I don't care if people at a reading understand me or not. I want to be like a waterfall that cascades over them," and this idea of irreverence toward the audience had been one that seemed to permeate the American literary reading landscape.

When writers were sometimes funny, the crowd sat silent, unsure of whether they were allowed to laugh. They were cemented to their uncomfortable folding chairs like children with no agency, surrounded by people not here for the reading but to peruse a bookstore or be seen perusing in a bookstore. This room was full of loud conversations and cash registers and the occasional wailing child.

The event was pretty lackluster, and we tried to do our best to pretend it wasn't. But no matter how hard I tried, I thought to myself, *This kind of sucks.*

I don't know why people even go to readings sometimes, except to meet others in their tribe, which is to say masochists.

By the time I got up, I knew my work would not be received well. I wasn't here to talk about injustice because people can only perceive one kind of packaged injustice at a time. And 2015 Brooklyn was not the time. I wasn't here to be cool because I know I'm not cool. I wasn't here to make friends because I know these are not my people—nor are they people I want to spend time with outside of my work environment, which is what I consider this.

Honestly, I didn't really even want to be there. And all I could think of as I walked up to the podium when it was my turn to read my poems about my grandma and all the ways people hurt sometimes and my great affinity for the work of the moon is *I can't believe I'm going to miss the first quarter of the WVU-Oklahoma football game for this.*

And then I read my poems about my grandma and told some jokes and talked about hurt and the great work of the moon, and a couple people laughed and the people who were in the bookstore to find books talked loudly and found their books and I did my best to make it through. After the reading, I ran over to the person who put it on and said, "Thank you for having me and publishing my poems. I have to go, but it was wonderful being part of this."

I ran out of the bookstore and into the night searching for a bar. By the time I found one, there was only six minutes left in the second quarter and West Virginia was down big and I looked around at all the people, some who had their heads down, some who were watching the game, others talking to the bartender, all of us holding on to some hurt or another and I thought, *Now these are my people.*

THE NEXT morning I woke to an email that read, *I was at the reading you did last night and I loved the way you talked about the moon and your grandma and I think you'd make a great addition to our little family. Would you consider coming to one of our readings and experience it before you make a decision?*

There was no football game that night, so I went.

THE FIRST time I walked down the alley tucked off of Norfolk street, I was just like you.

And when I climbed up those industrial steps, the large

door man said, "ID?" and then checked my ID and my name was on a list and he said, "Alright, go on in."

The door opened up onto a scene I'd never have believed had I not seen it with my own eyes.

Through the door I stumbled upon what looked like a party straight out of *The Great Gatsby* or a salon at Gertrude Stein's home in Paris. There were dancers and costumes and people punching typewriter keys. There were public poetry readings and a jazz singer. It was an immersive reading that felt more like a party. Like a world created for the reading to exist in.

Everyone looked beautiful and was dressed up, and it was as if I had stumbled upon a secret I wasn't supposed to know.

This place was called the Poetry Brothel, which was a 1920s-themed party that allowed patrons who enjoyed a poet's public reading to then be led to the back of the room where there was a bookshelf with a secret door that could be opened and you would find yourself in another room, draped in pearls and velvet and candlelight, where for poker chips, purchased from the Madame, you could purchase an intimate one-on-one reading with a poet of your liking.

This immersive experience allowed the context for the poems to take on a whole other life. There were no podiums. There was no line to divide artists from patrons. And for the first time in my life, I felt like there was a vision of my art form, which could be experienced and fleshed out in the present. Lacking the cynicism, righteousness, and ladder climbing of the various American poetry scenes, this place changed the focus of what a reading was derived for and made it more about entertaining and moving people and making them think, which is what I thought art was supposed to be.

It's easier to convince someone of a truth if you can meet them in the middle by entertaining them. Had you been in the room that night, you would have believed too.

That was how I was folded into my poetry brothel family,

with artists and writers and contortionists and illusionists and tarot readers.

Ernest Pettaway could do things I couldn't do in real life. He was charming and fearless and lived in a brothel. The alter ego found things in my life that could be utilized in performance and exaggerated them so I could convince others.

It was the first time I felt a real connection to the magic people speak of when they talk about this city, where anything is possible. A city where things can exist, that can't exist anywhere else.

And so, behind the doors of this New York City speakeasy, for better or worse, I was becoming some concentrated form of myself. It was like when Paul, John, Ringo, and George went to Hamburg, Germany, and left the Beatles. I cut my teeth there. I learned to be funny on stage. I learned to write for an audience. I finally had one to write for. I was making a new family.

Before each show, I would walk into the venue as Keegan, and I would remove my clothes in the dressing room and strip down, as a handful of others stripped down, as burlesque dancers walked backstage naked, and the Madame layered on her makeup, and the magician in his street clothes transformed beneath his suit and bow tie, as the contortionists practiced pretzeling their bodies and an adjunct NYU drama teacher transformed into the master of ceremonies, warming up his voice with scales and working his fingers across his accordion and as we then emerged from behind the hidden trap door, from behind this bookshelf, onto the stage, we were no longer the people who'd walked into a speakeasy minutes prior—but one of the blooming lights making New York, New York.

my flatbush friends

....

They were there when I moved into the building off of Flatbush Avenue in the fall of 2014, after escaping my roommate who would not let me use the shower or kitchen, who lit a hundred candles in the living room and stared into them after I told him I was going to report him to the police for stealing my credit card information. Who, as I moved out of the apartment, was passed out on his fold-out bed in the living room next to two empty bottles of chardonnay covered with colorful animals leaping all over the bottle.

They were smoking a joint, wearing T-shirts that accentuated their muscles, and were friendly as can be, "Can we give you a hand, man?" one said, leaning against a wall of the stairwell.

"Sure, thanks," I said.

Often, they were on my floor or just below it in the stairwell smoking a joint when I was leaving or coming home. They were smoking a joint mornings I ran out the house for job interviews and smoking nights when I came back from readings and from doing my laundry. They were smoking in the stairwell months where I was broke and months where I was heartbroken, and months I was so numb I couldn't feel nothing at all. The kind of months I missed home and I kept sayin' to myself, *You can't go there. You can't go home 'cause you aren't from anywhere*, and I'd walk by them and we'd smile at each other.

AND THIS one blizzard a couple winters back I went out for ice cream. I said, "Eric."

Eric was my new roommate. "Eric, it's shitting snow out there. It looks like the snow apocalypse and I'm not gonna get caught dead on the five p.m. news in this apartment without some peanut butter and chocolate ice cream in my stomach."

"Alright, Keegan," he said in the tone he often used with me, which was kind but also a mixture of disbelief and a pinch patronizing. Eric was finishing his PhD in French experimental poetry, so you know the tone I'm talking about, though he's a good guy.

They were in the stairwell that night too, window cracked, smoking a joint. "Shit, you aren't going out there, are you?" one of them said. I nodded and smiled, as I walked down and out into the white.

Outside, everything was still except for the wind. It was so cold. It was the kind of cold when everything is clear. The kind of cold when everything comes into focus. The night was clear, yet heavy like carrying a large bag of water on your shoulders and in your lungs.

Everything around me was turned off except a few lights overhead from the apartment buildings, a scatter of bodegas and my Dunkin' Donuts/Baskin Robbins.

"How are the roads?" the woman behind the register asked when I walked into Dunkin' Donuts.

"Pretty bad. I don't think you can drive them or anyone can drive them, I mean, uh, ma'am."

"Coffee?"

"Nah, I'm more interested in your ice cream. Can I get two pints of your peanut butter and chocolate?"

She made a face, but I didn't care. I could eat whatever I

wanted in a snowstorm. *I'm a grown ass man*, I wanted to say. *Take your judging butt home*, I wanted to say, which I knew she couldn't even do because there was a snowstorm afoot and plus she probably had to work.

"I was wondering 'cause my replacement never showed up tonight and I've been on for nearly thirteen hours."

I feel bad for being an asshole in my head.

"SHIT, HE did it," one of the guys smoking in the stairwell said. "You gotta try this," another one said.

So, of course, I tried it. Who's gonna turn down free weed during a snowstorm, especially one of this magnitude?

And you know what? It was just okay.

"Thanks, guys," I said and dragged my snowy body up three more flights of stairs and into my apartment.

I ATE nearly an entire pint of ice cream that night, nodding off to an episode of ESPN's *30 for 30*. It's the one where Ohio State completely screws over Maurice Clarett. The reason the documentary is so good is that it was able to capture people being evil who have no idea they're being evil while they do the evil things they do out in the open. It helps that the little sweater-vest-wearing coach from Ohio State doesn't realize he's evil. The athletic director does not know he's evil either or maybe he does. It's hard to tell. But there are cameras everywhere catching them both being evil. Only, the camera also captures Maurice Clarett forgiving them and going back to them again and again, trying to survive multiple systems that were conceived to downplay his greatness and brilliance and personhood. He keeps going back to them because he says that they're like family.

This is my go-to documentary when I'm high and in an apocalyptic snowstorm. Every single time I watch this *30 for 30*, I say, *Keegan, we are going to quit watching football*. But I never do. And Maurice Clarett might not realize it, but his sweater-vest-wearing coach is a bad guy. It's easy to see that his AD is bad. Every time that guy lies or is angry, a vein bulges from his forehead so big I think it might explode. Like when he says, *Hi, I care about the well-being of our student athletes at Ohio State,* his vein looks like a balloon about to burst. Sometimes I have to close my eyes because it looks like the vein in his head is going to explode and even though he's evil, no one wants to see someone die from an aneurysm mid *30 for 30*.

Maurice Clarett keeps going back to his coach and I keep going back to football and we're both screwed.

THEY WERE in the stairwell smoking when I'd leave for Brighton Beach Tuesdays, the summer my friend Judy and I went to Brighton Beach almost every week because we both needed something to look forward to.

Our weekly tradition started on Cinco de Mayo. Cinco de Mayo is this American holiday where people get drunk and celebrate Mexico winning the Battle of Puebla because Mexico was better at not getting malaria than their French conquering counterparts. We celebrate this every year, even though Mexico ultimately loses the war to France. It's a strange holiday to think about, but probably no stranger than St. Patrick's Day, which is a day we celebrate in America by drinking because this British guy named Pat brought Christianity to a largely Druid population of Ireland, which was doing just fine, and said, *Let's get a bunch of people to fight over their idea of the same religion for the next eight hundred years to make it easier to control a British Colony.* And guess what, it worked.

Our Brighton Beach Tuesdays started on Cinco de Mayo. It started with a fist of tacos and a margarita at a place a couple subway stops from my apartment.

"Hey, we're only a couple stops away from Brighton Beach," she said.

So we went to Brighton Beach.

EVERYTHING AT Brighton Beach was in Russian. I knew very little about Brighton Beach before we went, but I knew things might be in Russian. I did not know the extent to which everything would be in Russian. It was awesome.

We were walking around the beach town looking for bars and instead we find a strange old people's home right on the beach.

"This is where I want to be a convalescent," Judy said.

"Do you know the STD rates at places like that?" I said. "It's nuts."

"Guess there's not much else to do before you die."

AND SHE'S right. So we kept walking until we found this restaurant/café/bar/nightclub that must have been run by the mob. It was called Tatiana's. We walked through a nightclub entrance and it was decorated the way I'd assume a prom decorated by the mob might be decorated. It opened up into a corridor filled with creepy pictures on the wall, full of mobster-looking people standing next to a powerful-looking woman, who I assume was Tatiana. And there was one picture with Tatiana and a much younger Hillary Clinton. And there was one with Tatiana and Ray Charles. And there was one with Tatiana and Donald Trump and Bill Clinton, and the three of them look like they were just shooting the shit.

So we did what you do when you are in a long creepy corridor with pictures of mobsters and powerful women like Tatiana and Hillary Clinton: we kept walking toward the flickering neon light at the end of the hallway.

At the end of the hallway was a staircase. Judy looked at me like, *What do we do now?* And I looked back at her like, *We are so climbing those steps because whatever we encounter, I am nearly certain I can outrun you and likely will be okay.*

At least I think I got all that across with the look. She gave me the nod and we slowly scaled the staircase. The railing had Christmas lights snaking it and the step tiles changed colors every few seconds: *purple, magenta, lilac, pink, red.*

I'm color-blind though, so I only saw orange and blue tones.

WE WENT up and up and up a flight of stairs and then stepped into the light. We found ourselves in a café on the boardwalk. And there it was. Brighton Beach, just sitting all majestic and beachy out there in front of us. And there was the ocean. And I guess I can admit this here, but I started missing the Pacific.

We ordered drinks that arrived in jumbo glasses and got a little bit tipsier than we already were. Then Judy and I finished our drinks and walked out onto the beach and it was May so the sand was freezing cold, but we were tipsy so little mattered.

At some point we just plopped our tipsy selves down into the sand and drift and drift and drift like a plastic bag in the air, which is a metaphor and also something we literally saw before falling asleep in the cold sand of Brighton Beach.

"WHAT THE fuck?" a voice yelled out as if over a loudspeaker, startling me awake from my nap.

"Fuck you and your dog," another voice in a thick accent responded.

At the time I thought, *What could be better than this*? At the time I thought, *This is going to be great. There's no downside to this. I want to see where this goes.*

But it wasn't great. Not even a little. They just postured a little and then walked away and Judy and I decided on Cuban for dinner and so we both went home to change out of our Cinco de Mayo beach clothes and when I got into my stairwell one of the guys said, "Hey, you got a lighter?" and I did so I said, "Yeah," and handed him my lighter. He'd do the same for me. We're building neighbors after all. When I came back after changing, they weren't there anymore.

ONE DAY I met a girl. We started dating. Well, sorta. After six months of doing things that were date-like, she agreed to date me. A little after that she'd come to stay at my place every now and then and she'd always be like, "Who are those people smoking in the stairwell?"

"Oh, those are just the guys," I'd say.

ONE DAY I stayed over at her place. We both noticed it was much nicer than mine. Like way nicer. There were no mice, no roaches, nor strange phantom wall odors. All the lights worked and hardly any fungus grew above her shower head or in her kitchen. No one banged from the other side of her bedroom wall with a baseball bat or kept their music's bass blasting until 4:00 a.m.

And then a month later I found myself at her place a bunch. And then it turned two months later and I was at her place even more and then I was only coming to my apartment to grab things here and there and then I was only coming to my apartment to pay rent and then today is the day I'm moving out of my apartment.

"Shoulda told us you were moving," one of the guys says. "I got a van and everything."

"We would have helped ya," another said while smoking a joint.

I move my boxes into the foyer of the building. "I wish I would have known a couple weeks ago," I say.

"Are you getting kicked out?"

"Nah, my lease is just up."

"Oh okay. Does the super know?"

"Just the landlord."

"Yeah, they're trying to kick people out of their homes and flip the apartments. I think we get another six months."

From the way he says *home*, I realize the guys are just kids. Just trying to hold on to their home, because people are gentrifying their neighborhood. I was part of that.

They have a home, which is something I don't.

"Would you leave us a key?" one of the guys says.

I look at them, I'm sure the way my roommate Eric used to look at me.

"So we can smoke in your place and, uh, do other things until they finish renovating it?"

"Sure," I say. "I have a couple extra sets. I'll leave it under the mat."

"Thanks."

ON THE way out of the building for the last time, I'm all sweaty and thirsty after moving boxes, so I go to the bodega three storefronts down for Gatorade, only it wasn't the same bodega I'd been going to for the last two and a half years. There was a new glass facade and a new heavy door that shut slowly and new shiny aisles and gluten-free everything and vegan options and no bodega cats running around. *They even have low-calorie Gatorade.*

"When did you guys start renovating?" I ask the cashier.

"Oh, we took this over in February. Since late February."

"Wow. The neighborhood's beginning to change. Ever since they reopened Kings Theatre," I said.

"It's changing for the better. I used to work at the market down Flatbush and I seen it too. It's getting better," the cashier says.

And I wonder what that means. And I wonder because I only came for a short time and am leaving and even in the last seven months though my stuff was here, I did not live here. I wonder about what my presence has done to this neighborhood. I wonder if this is the cashier's neighborhood. I wonder about the teens in my building who have probably always lived in that building and know no other home. And I wonder if they know they're probably the best neighbors I've ever had.

west virginia day

....

The night I moved out of the apartment from the roommate who would not let me shower or cook, who had stolen my credit card information and demanded I share my bedroom with his cat, a cat who loved to do what cats love to do which is climb up to a ledge and with their cat paws nudge objects off the ledge and onto the floor, which is how I lost my favorite coffee mug and my favorite cologne, my roommate lit up the living room, which doubled as his bedroom, with veladoras. All sorts of candles with different depictions of the Virgin Mary. He said nothing at all. It was simultaneously one of the most beautiful and horrifying images I can conjure from my own life. And I knew it would only take one cat paw for everything to burn.

It took me two days to get everything out of my room and across the five or six blocks to my new apartment by myself.

I reached out to folks to see if I could get help and no one responded. None of my bartenders, none of the writers or any of my Facebook friends. One friend helped me make my last three trips, one in which we took my mattress, another in which we took my box spring, and the final in which I took all of my heaviest things and put them into a cab and we went five blocks and then carried all the boxes up into my new room, where I passed out exhausted from the last three days of work and my previous roommate.

THE FRIEND who helped me on the last three trips had gone to college with me in Morgantown and had moved to Brooklyn after finishing grad school in London, after meandering in DC for a month or so.

For some reason he hated New York City. Not because it was too much city but because it wasn't enough London for him. He began scheming all kinds of ways to get back to London.

"Keegan," he said one day, " I'm gonna go work in Africa and hopefully get hired from there to work in London on a job visa."

"That sounds like an idea," I said.

Eight months later, in the spring, he was hired by a company in Rwanda. He might have been the happiest person I've ever heard saying the words, "I'm moving to Rwanda at the end of the summer!"

All spring and all summer he kept throwing himself going away parties and I didn't mind it because any reason is a good reason to celebrate a friend. At one of these parties, it was just the two of us and all of Williamsburg, Brooklyn, sitting out on a blacktop playground of a local elementary school for a preview of *Wet Hot American Summer*, a brand-new Netflix series that was supposed to be based on the movie.

The television show was shit though.

As we sat there, watching this terrible show, with all the other hipsters, I thought on how my last friend in New York was moving away. I should have said, *I'm gonna miss you*, or *I know you'll make it to London someday*, or *I'm glad you're going to pursue your dream*. Instead I said, "This show is terrible. I'm gonna go get some tacos from the taco truck. Would you like some tacos?"

"Yeah, grab me a couple carne asada."

"No problem."

As I walked to the taco truck I took in all the hip things around me. The fixie bikes and handlebar mustaches and the parents walking their children on leashes. The sun had just set and it was one of the first times I'd been outside in shorts this year. I'm sure the stars were out but I couldn't tell.

I CHECKED my email to see if my writing had been rejected by anywhere today and instead of a rejection or a discount code or an email about how if I sign this petition I could be *the real change in the world*, I received an email from Howard Parsons, the high school boyfriend of my best friend, Courtney.

Hey, bud. Me and some people are thinking about doing a tour in West Virginia with writers and artists and musicians. Would you like to come?

AND THEN things started changing.

....

A few months later I'm back in Morgantown and it's summer and the cardinals are flying and the rain is pouring and I'm nervous as hell, which isn't unusual, but this time it's because I'm about to hop into a tour van, which is new.

Howard and I were the writers on tour. Tyler Grady, David Bello, and John R. Miller were the musicians. Bryan Richards was the visual artist and merch guy. We all went back at least ten years, and as I stepped foot into the tour van, I was thinking, *Dear God, I hope we don't die.*

Our first show was at a Latin American restaurant in Elkins, West Virginia, which doubled as a music venue. A local, Mike Burgess, who'd just had a baby was there to interview us for a podcast he was working on. The restaurant fed us and gave us drinks for free. The owner said, "I wish more people were doing things like this. We need more Traveling West Virginia Arts."

Then we all performed. It was the first night so we were all a little rusty, working to find our groove and it wasn't super packed by any means. That night I thought I did alright, but looking back, I probably sucked.

No, I for sure sucked.

When Dave sang, it reminded me of being young. Eighteen or nineteen at 123 Pleasant Street in Morgantown, when people still smoked in the music venue and he would sing a song he wrote called "Two," and everyone would sing and scream along. Few days have gone by in my life when I haven't thought of his lyrics: "And you said to me / Will you remember me when I'm famous / And I said to you / I'll never be famous / Because I'm nothing / If not honest, and I'll always be nothin', I can see myself at thirty with a wife and some kids / and a house and a car / and I don't think that I really want to die there / but I don't think I got a choice." They haunted me then and still haunt me now. Dave's band, The

World Is a Beautiful Place and I'm No Longer Afraid to Die, tours the world now. He has indeed become famous.

John intimidated the hell out of me. I knew him in undergrad but was afraid of him. We met one night when someone whisked me away from a block party near my dorm, taking me on a near mile walk to meet him just because I casually said *I love music* to a stranger at the party. When I got there he was sitting in a bedroom on the edge of a bed singing songs to a handful of people and he handed me his guitar but I was too drunk and not talented enough to do anything with it so he just went back to playing again and I thought this might be the most talented human I've ever met. When he plays, you feel what he feels more than you hear any kind of sound. And that hasn't changed. He understands a room and has impeccable timing. He can do anything performance-wise and can captivate people.

Howard got up and read and he was nervous as hell, because he gets nervous in front of people. His story was really good though and the audience laughed and gasped along.

Tyler was great too. He has one of the best rock-and-roll voices I've ever heard. He's also just a huge force, and I stopped worrying so much that I would die when I was around him.

Bryan's zine had little pieces of all of our work in it and I couldn't believe that I got to be among all these people that mean so much to me.

AFTER WE shut down the bar of this Latin restaurant and Mike could no longer interview us in the alleyway because we were too loud, we went to another bar with a pool table. We shot some pool and talked about how much we all love West Virginia, and for the first time in a long time I did not feel alone.

The next couple shows were good and bad and mostly good. People would take us to their favorite restaurants and swimming holes. We made a pilgrimage to Bob's Hot Dogs, this stand where there were a hundred ways to dress your hot dogs. We had a science field trip at the Green Bank Observatory Science Center. We had stragglers who decided to just hop into the van and go from town to town with us. People who would blow off work to be part of this.

One of them was Sophia, a barista who I met in Morgantown years ago, who the first night I met her sang me the most beautiful songs on her front porch. They were quirky and kind and always searching for answers and never confident that there is a singular worldview or perception. Her songs knew everything could be impacted or muddled by something else. Her music had all the pieces to it that made me first fall in love with poetry.

By the time we got to our show in Lewisburg at Hill and Holler, we'd all settled into our routines. That day was also the day I was gonna meet my hero Scott McClanahan.

We got to the venue very, very early. We noticed that it was a restaurant, which at that point in the tour we'd realized were not good venues for what we were doing. With not much to do, we started day drinking. Then someone who wasn't drinking drove us out to their favorite swimming hole just five miles out of town and a half mile hike into the woods. Everyone hopped into the shallow part of the river. It smelled like summer. It had been raining most of the mornings we'd been on the road. A couple kayakers passed us. It felt like when we stood up and walked out of the water, like we'd become something else. Like we were leaving the waters as a family and were no longer these singular creative sparks but together something luminous. It was as if we were all new people, and this was our family now.

We got back into the van and went back to the venue. Apparently this was also the grand opening of the restaurant, so there was supposed to be a ton of people. And little by little, a ton of people started showing up.

WHEN I saw Scott, I was too afraid to talk to him. So I went back to the van and had another drink and tried to sort out whatever it was I was gonna read that night. I ran into two friends from college in the parking lot, and they'd just had their first baby. Last time I saw them they were raising ferrets and I had ended up sleeping in a sheet and pillow fort they built in their living room, for whatever reason, even though my apartment was only a block from theirs. They'd come to Greenbrier County to slow down and begin life. And I felt like I hadn't the faintest idea how to do that.

I picked out some poems and had another drink of vodka chased with orange juice, which John had named "mouth driver" earlier that day. The orange juice wasn't cold anymore and someone had left their wet clothes in the van and the van began to smell like a corpse, so I walked back to the venue and tried to rub the corpse stink off me.

"It's so good to finally meet you, Scott. Your book means the world to me" is how I introduced myself to him.

"Aw, thank you," he said.

Then I ran away back to the van.

THEN IT was time for me to go on and so I thought I would try to read my best/funniest stuff. When I got on stage, the room was full of people and people were going in and out and onto the back patio. It was a large room with a stage. Maybe there shouldn't have been a stage in that room though. The bulk of people were there to try out this new restaurant that just opened and had no want for a poet. It's not like a musician who can sneak into the background and just flood your consciousness and make you feel things mid-conversation.

It was loud when I got on stage and only got louder as I read. It continued to get louder and louder and louder and I'm sure I sucked.

Tyler kept walking, looking around mad, and John looked

mad and Howard was pacing. I thought, *I must really be sucking.*

I ended by saying very meagerly, "And I'm so excited to be reading tonight with one of my heroes, Scott *McClane*."

I'm not sure if I butchered his name because I'd been drinking mouth drivers or if it was because I was very afraid or because everything felt like it was going wrong in that moment. But in front of seventy strangers who just wanted to try out a new restaurant and instead had to listen to me read poems about my grandma and orcas and about what people do to each other sometimes, I butchered my hero's name pretty good.

A faint scatter of applause applauded as I ran off stage and straight to the van for another mouth driver. Someone else had beat me to it though. We were all out of vodka and orange juice. I left the sliding door open to get the corpse smell of out of the van. My friends from college came up and said, *You did real good,* and *We're going to head home and take care of the baby.*

I gave them hugs. "Hope I see you two soon," I said.

Howard came by. "Any mouth driver supplies left?"

"Nope. We're all out."

"Aw. Shit. Okay."

"When do you go up?"

"Soon. Tyler and John were furious about all the talking when you were up there."

"Yeah?" I said, a little surprised that anyone even cared about me.

"They were trying to get everyone to shut up."

"Restaurants."

"Restaurants."

"Good luck," I said.

"Thank you." And then Howard looked in a couple of places I hadn't tried and found a few hidden bottles stowed away. One was tequila and one was whiskey. We each pulled on the tequila and went back to the venue.

BY THE time Scott took the stage, hardly anyone was left. Maybe thirty people. Everyone got out of their seats and moved up to the front. I took my shoes off and sat on the floor next to the stage, next to a basket of flowers someone brought us. Sophia came and sat next to me and then Howard and then some other folks. Hannah, who was friends with everyone on the tour, one of the folks who hopped into our van after the second show and never left, came up too. She leaned over and whispered into my ear, *This is gonna be real good.*

When I read poems, I'm very quiet. Often afraid. My reading voice is me but doesn't sound like me, or like the magic well from which my poems come. Now when Scott reads, it's something that is only him. First he doesn't read as much as he preaches. He's almost shouting into the microphone, the way a preacher on the corner might shout and his cadences are so beautiful and of himself that you hang on to every single word. It feels more like someone telling you a story than someone reading you a story. It feels like you are in the story too. It's funny and sad and you will understand all the words. He uses simple beautiful words like *shit* and *love* and *grandma* to explain some of the world's most complicated things. In the middle of his story there's a part about fudge and out of nowhere he has a bowl of fudge brownies that he unwraps and just starts passing out to the audience. It's like watching a live jazz band and the music can move in any direction depending on a look or a nod. And now you become the music too.

Sitting there with my friends, my family, in the place I love, listening to my favorite writer ever, I knew what I wanted to do with my life. I wanted to entertain people. I wanted to bring people together. I wanted to stop writing for myself and to write for others.

After the reading, Scott signed my book and I realized how shitty my performance was compared to his, how bad every one of my readings this tour must have been. How I didn't have enough conviction in my work to even yell the words that I wrote, as if I meant them the way he means them. And as I thought on all these things, he handed me my book back and I ran into a corner where no one could see me, and I looked at what he'd written.

He'd written, *I like your poems.*

....

After the show, Sophia took us to her family's yurt—which was out in the middle of nowhere. We stopped at a liquor store and got some beer and ciders and drove out into the woods. We kept driving until the roads stopped being roads. Until they were just dirt. And then we drove some more. When we got to where we were going, there were more stars in the sky than I'd ever seen before.

We got a campfire started. Bryan started telling ghost stories the way he does, and we howled at the moon the way we do.

In the morning, no one had very good reception unless you were out on the trampoline. So a few of us walked over to the trampoline. There was a big pond right next to it with long whiskered catfish swimming around kissing each other with their catfish whiskers.

As our phones started getting notifications we found out that while we slept, a man in South Carolina walked into a Black church and killed nine people.

Suddenly everything seemed small in comparison: my roommate stealing my credit card information and attempting to starve me, my broken mug and cologne, his cat, my only friend in New York City moving to Africa, my homesickness, my inability to publish, my mispronunciation of my hero's name in front of my hero and a room full of folks, my heart sickness, my autoimmune disorder, my grandma's loneliness, my fear of being around people, my inability to find work and my running out of money, because for now I am still alive and there are others who are far better humans than I who are not granted that.

THE LAST five years I've spent West Virginia Day with my friends in West Virginia. When I think of West Virginia Day, I think of Andrea Null years and years ago telling me in the

Apothecary, *Of course I'll drive three hours out of the way from Charleston to pick you up, so we can go see Elaine McMillion's Hollow Project debut in Welch.* I think of how a few days after sitting on that trampoline, the day after West Virginia Day, I woke up on a couch in Shepherdstown, West Virginia, and I tiptoed up some creaky old steps in an old house to find all of my favorite people piled upon each other in a massive cuddle puddle in a bedroom. Because of these people and this place, I will always have a home. I want to find a way to entertain my friends and strangers, to write with enough conviction that I can yell each and every word I write. I want to help others live a little more during the short time we have here. I took a picture of them all piled up because I knew I needed something to remind me of this day and this family for all the other kinds of days ahead of me.

part four

tour diary: day off
in morgantown

....

Howard is sitting in his truck. Adam is in the front seat, looking out the front window thinking about life, or someone in Huntington, West Virginia, or someone in Ohio, or someone in New York City or his mom and dad in Los Angeles and packing up his childhood home because in a few weeks they'll be moving from Los Angeles to Atlanta. Or maybe he is thinking *how the hell will I finish my book*. It's always hard to pin exactly what Adam's thinking about, but right then he is looking forward and the only thing in front of him is Howard's mom's tomato garden and a red shed.

Everyone else piles into the truck bed. Darrin hops into the truck bed. Then Kevin hops into the truck bed. Then Sophia jumps into the truck bed and I look at all of them like, *Y'all are crazy, that's how Chris Henry died.*

Slowly I make my way around to the driver's side window and say, "Howard, can I sneak into the back seat?"

"Sure, man."

ADAM GETS out of the front seat and we push a bunch of crap to one side of the truck and I burrow in next to a cooler full of beer and sleeping bags and books and old outlaw country tape cassettes and what looks like an endless supply of empty beef jerky packets and a single Mexican yarn blanket. I slide open the back window and start taking pictures of Kevin and

Darrin and Soph who are all smiling and enjoying themselves as we peel out of Howard's neighborhood and head down the mountain toward the lake. The sun is falling down on their faces and their skin, and the wind is blowing in their hair, making them all look like models. I can't hear what they're talking about but the way they smile makes it seem like it's some kind of beautiful secret. It could have been anything. It was probably, *What kind of hot dogs you gonna get in Fairmont tomorrow before the show?*

When we stop winding down the hill, the lake is all around us. It's like it comes out of nowhere. It's just lake and blue sky and clouds and more lake. We cross a bridge and boats are everywhere. There are people inner-tubing behind boats and jet-skiing and enjoying the sun. The three of them in the back of the truck bed look like models and I can't stop thinking, *Man, that's how Chris Henry died.*

We get out of the truck and wind down a trail to the lake, and the woods now surround us and strangers, who are smiling, surround us and they are a little drunk and a little high and some stranger dogs and some strangers with coolers and some strangers with shirts on and some strangers with their shirts off are walking toward where they are headed and everyone is headed forward.

At the edge of the lake, there's a little rock jetty that protrudes out like a thumb. We drop all of our stuff at the shore's brim, and people start taking off their clothes, stripping down to bathing suits and underwear.

Adam and I are hesitant. See, Adam and I are the writers on this tour, which is way different from being a rock and roller. The rock and rollers just run out and do things. They're fearless.

THIS ONE time last year on tour one of the rock and rollers, Jake, had river shoes, which are shoes you put on your feet so you don't cut up your feet on glass or on a car that someone decided to drive into the river and hide a dead body in. And after our show in Thomas, West Virginia, we got asked to go to a bonfire and the people said, "You'll smell it before you see it," and they were right. After walking a mile or so into the darkness away from town, down some railroad tracks along the Black Water River, we smelled some fire. But we couldn't see shit because it was dark as hell and the fire was hidden a little bit by a thicket of brush. We were still another two-thirds of a mile away and I thought, *Shit, we'll never find it.* But that's because I'm a writer. The rock and rollers had complete confidence. And they were right. And a little while later we found it. When we got there, someone said, "Let's all go skinny-dipping in the river," and Jake was like, "Hell, yeah," and some other rock and rollers on the tour were like, "Hell, yeah," and Adam and I found a nice log and sat down and played with the dog, because that's what we do on tour. A little while later we heard howling at the moon. It was Jake. And Jake walked up to us, his foot all bloody and I was like, "Jake, why didn't you wear your river shoes?" and Jake just shrugged and kept howling at the moon like a rock and roller would, bleeding all over the place.

So THIS year, Adam and I were excited that Kevin was going to be on tour with us because he's a writer and we needed to increase our numbers. But Kevin is rock and roll as hell too.

If you ever catch him playing banjo or even just overhear him speaking, you're like, *I think someone 'bout killed all the Rolling Stones and made them reincarnate into the body of this boy from Elkins.* Of course he doesn't have all the weird baggage of the Rolling Stones either. He just feels and does. If you asked him, he'd probably say, "Fuck the Rolling Stones," and he'd be right.

He always starts out like us. Like, *Guys I'm not sure about this.* And then Darrin, a rock and roller, says, "COMEEEON"

and it's as if the words *come on*, if said correctly, are magic
or something because then Kevin does whatever scary thing
we writers are all afraid of.

Not this time. The moment Kevin sees the rope swing at
the edge of the lake, he doesn't need any encouragement. He
grabs the rope and he looks at it a moment like a scientist and
then he looks at the lake and then back at the rope and then
at the lake and then at a rock near the lake's edge and then
SWOOOOOOOOSH he's gone. Then he swims back to the
lake bank and does it again. *SWOOOOOOOOSH*. And again
SWOOOOOOOOSH and again until it was like none of us
were even there. And then Darrin tries it. *SWOOOOOOOOSH*
into the lake. And then Kevin and then Darrin again.

Howard and Soph jump into the lake from the end of the
rock thumb jetty. They look like they're having fun. I take
my shirt off. I look at Adam. I give Adam a look that means,
I think I'm gonna try this lake thing, and he gives me a look
that says, *We aren't close enough yet where I understand
what all your looks mean*. Then out loud he says, "I don't
know what you're trying to do with your eyes." So I say,
"Adam, I think I'm gonna try this lake thing," and he says,
"Oh, cool. I thought you were looking for sunscreen. I don't
have any sunscreen. I'm just gonna stay here and take it easy
peasy and read this Camus."

And he did.

*SWOOOOOOOOSH SWOOOOOOOOSH SWOOOOOOOOSH
SWOOOOOOOOSH*

Kevin is still swinging into the lake. Howard and Soph and
Darrin are treading water with their Miller heavy cans floating around them like tugboats.

Now I am a little buzzed on whiskey at that point because
I drank at the house before we came, because beer makes me
sick and I was worried about how to bring whiskey down to
a lake because I worry about everything, but right then I'm

not as worried as usual because I'm a little whiskey-buzzed, so I jump into the lake. And you know what? I didn't die.

This is a huge life development. I swim left. I swim right. I'm still not dead.

The sun cascading down feels warm on my skin and I couldn't remember the last time I had this much skin out in the sun and maybe that's what's wrong with me.

I touch the slimy bottom of the lake with my toes. This scares me, but I'm not dead. I swim out far enough that I can't touch the bottom anymore and this scares me too, but I'm not dead. Speedboats speed off in the distance and I still am not dead. The trees line the rolling hills on the banks of the lake and are majestic and everything feels like it's touching me.

SWOOOOOOOOSH SWOOOOOOOOSH SWOOOO OOOOSH

"Screw it," I say to no one, which is what happens when you're a little scared and a little whiskey-buzzed in a lake.

I climb out of the water onto the rocky thumb jetty and shimmy across the bank of the lake to Kevin. Kevin hands me the rope swing. I look at it a moment like a scientist and then I look at the lake and then back at the rope and then at the lake and then at a rock near the lake's edge and then I close my eyes and then open them and then *SWOOOOOOOOSH*. I'm gone, but not dead.

The old me that was afraid is gone too. Somehow I can see what I couldn't see before. *It's like duende but with a tree swing*, I think to myself, which is exactly what a whiskey-buzzed writer would think.

Then Kevin and I just swing from the rope swing until it's time to go.

We walk back up through the forest and the strangers don't look like strangers anymore. They look like friends. We climb up the mountain and up through the trees and over rocks and over some fallen tree trunks and up a flight of stairs and then to the parking lot.

Howard gets into the front seat. Darrin hops into the truck bed and then Kevin hops in and then Sophia. Adam has the front passenger door open, looking at me.

"Nah. I'm gonna jump into the back," I say.

"Easy peasy," Adam says.

WE START driving and it's not scary at all. And the wind is in our faces and my shirt is still off and the sun is coming down and for the first time in my life, I feel like I'm beautiful, like the others. Like my mother and father and sister and my friends and strangers, like West Virginia. I'm smiling for the first time in a long time.

And then the truck stops.

"Shit. We're gonna be stuck behind this light that takes forever," Howard hollers back through the open cab window that I'd been taking pictures through earlier.

And I'm not sure why, but Kevin just stands up. Kevin starts flapping his arms like a bird. Like he is gonna just take off right then and there and fly back home. *KAAAAA Ka KAAAAA Ka KAAAAA Ka KAAAAA Ka KAAAAA Ka.* He is screaming like a bird or a Rolling Stone or a rock and roller or a writer or like Kevin.

And I believe him. I believe Kevin can fly away at any moment if he chooses, not because he's a rock and roller but because he's Kevin, a boy from Elkins, West Virginia, who was meant to fly.

my grandpa rice

....

On the airplane I turn to my dad who's sitting in his aisle seat trying to get internet on his phone. He's wearing Bose wireless headphones, which is an example of a good Christmas present.

This year I gave him a poem, like an idiot, and a fire pit, which he seemed happy with. And then my mom said, "Joe, you got another present under the tree," all excited like she just won Christmas and I thought, *Oh shit. This was gonna be the year where I'd get out of this alright.*

Then she walks over and hands him a box that was hidden from all the other boxes and he opens it and screams, "This is *just* what I wanted. How did you know?" the way people say it when pretending like they didn't just tell the person they live with what they actually want for Christmas.

I NUDGE my dad, sitting across the aisle and say, "You think Grandpa will come to the game? It's the first time our teams are playing each other in over a decade."

My dad looks at me like I'm an idiot. Then he looks a little sad and says, "No, Keegan. I don't think he's gonna come to the game."

....

And then we went to the game without my grandpa in a beautiful stadium in Orlando. And the University of Miami handed us our asses. Last night we stood beneath the bright stadium lights with my aunt and her husband who are Miami Hurricane fans. We were all wrapped up with good feelings and moved by the percussion and brass and symphony of the marching bands. And then we were blindsided by bad feelings and then disastrously bad feelings, as sometimes the unwritten script of sport will lend itself to.

And even though the University of Miami handed us our asses the night before, we got up really early the next morning and drove an hour and some change to see my grandpa and my grandma, who are both my mother's parents. Now we are sitting in a Tex-Mex restaurant in Melbourne, Florida, which if you've got grandparents living in Florida, you've probably been to both this Tex-Mex restaurant and Melbourne. There's likely a one in seven chance your grandparents live here too. Melbourne is essentially where grandparents go to drive dangerously. Grandma decided to stay at home, probably to avoid all the dangerous grandparents on the road, so it ends up just being Grandpa, my dad, and me out at lunch.

In the middle of lunch my dad gets up to use the restroom. And then it's just the two of us, my grandpa and me. And I'm sitting there not knowing what to say, but then I get real curious and so I ask what's been on my mind a long while.

"Grandpa, why'd you leave Ohio?"

" 'Cause it sucked," he laughs.

I laugh too and smile. I think to myself, *This guy is great.* I think, *Screw Ohio.*

"I'm sort of kidding, but not," he says. "I grew up in a place called Youngstown—"

"That's where Maurice Clarett and Jim Tressel are from."

"Yeah, there's a bunch of good football from there and I

looked around at all my friends and all the dads and all the people while I was growing up and they all said 'I want to graduate high school and get a job in this steel mill and live the life my parents lived.' I could see that one day the mill would die, but also, I just knew that life wasn't for me. At the time, all over the television I could see people were flying planes and trying to get into space, down in Florida. And I said I want to be like that. I want to be like those people. I want to fly planes. I want to go to space. And I guess I dreamed a bunch about going to space back then."

And this is the first time in my entire life I feel related to anyone in my family.

"I looked at the people all around me and I knew I didn't want to be like them," he says.

And my grandpa gives me a little smile.

When my dad returns from the bathroom, my grandfather starts in on some bullshit, the way he does when he talks to my father sometimes, and he says, "It sure looked like Skylar Howard couldn't see over the offensive line last night, Joe," with his crooked grin, flashing half his teeth, the way John Wayne did in the movies when he was pretending to be as suave as my grandpa actually is.

After the bill comes, I hug my grandpa and I hug him again before we walk to our cars and go our separate ways.

"Let's keep in touch better this time," I say, and he nods at me like he knows we are both lying, like I am a damned fool.

But then, no one wants to say to their grandfather, "I'll see you when I see you."

....

On the drive back to the airport I thought about how all the things making up my grandfather make me too. All our cells and blood and stardust. I thought about how we both love Ramsey Lewis and how he used to collect Columbia Records and was in a club where he got LPs mailed to him each month and how he'd always talk about being in the nightclubs in Miami when he was young and watching most of the greats pass through, as the greats always drift in and out of the nightclubs of our minds, and how I've done the same thing.

I thought about how he took me on a boat four or five years back to patrol the canals and inlet waterways of Melbourne, Florida, and we saw cranes and he said, "Keegan, that's an Egret over there," and we saw high grasses coming out of the water and the wind was making them dance and he said, "That's a mangrove. A bunch of fish live in the bottom there," and he was no bullshit as he patrolled the waters with his buddy in this old police boat that some organization let retired men patrol around in.

During my first year living in New York City, my first year in grad school, I'd stopped sleeping. No one ever tells you when you move to New York that you will see too much. You will see so much hurt and you will see too many homeless people and you will see homeless people shit on the subway and you will only see the foundations of buildings because we aren't all allowed to see the world from the tops and you will hurt your neck trying to look up at them and sometimes you will see and you will realize another world exists that you do not live in and that likely you will never live in. You will sit up in bed trying to turn your brain off to all the things you've seen and heard that day. And sometimes you can't. I couldn't.

On that trip, the drive from the airport in Orlando to their house in Melbourne made me feel like a human again. The airline lost my bag and all I had was a heavy Navy peacoat and pants and sweaters, to fight the bitter cold of the March New York I'd left. And all of a sudden I was in Florida, struggling to wrap my mind around so much open space.

A numbness was subsiding. The everglades and grasses and cranes were saving my life. It was just mile after mile of open everglade and nothing and my head did not know how to process it and I started crying in the back seat of the car as my grandfather drove us to his house.

MY GRANDFATHER continued naming things in the canal as his buddy went on about shit from the war, though it wasn't clear which war he was talking about. But he was saving my life too. I stood on the boat in the balmy Florida spring in my peacoat, because it was all I had, and then we'd see a rock in the water and my grandfather would say, "That's a manatee," pointing with his rolled up newspaper that he kept near him because he's always playing the crossword puzzle like a boss.

And we cruised the canals and inlets like that for a while and I for the first time in a long time said nothing at all. I just listened. I listened to my grandfather name all of these beautiful things and talk about marlin fishing and the old days in Miami. Then we went and shot the shit while we ate some diner food with his buddy at their place where the waitress knew their names and the cook knew their names and some folks passing by knew their names and I thought, *This is great.*

....

On the way back to the airport, after leaving the Tex-Mex restaurant and leaving my grandfather in the parking lot and leaving all the slow yet deadly golf carts of Melbourne, Florida, I start thinking about the stories my mother used to tell me about her dad. How her dad would take her and her sisters out fishing and camping when they were little, and they'd go water skiing too and it was almost as if they lived in a different time and a different America than the one my father grew up in. My grandfather was living the glamorous air traffic controller life at Miami International Airport, and my mom was born on an air force base because her mom was a super-top-secret military something. I thought about how everyone went on about how great my dad's father is, and people didn't say much about my mom's dad and I wonder if that's because when you're confident within yourself you don't need people talking you up. For whatever reason I've always been much closer with my dad's father, even though everything about me screams that I'm like my mother's. I wish I'd known there was this other person I was related to who wanted to name things like me. But you can't go back in time.

....

But let's go back in time anyway, to when I was young and my family visited my mom's parents a couple times out at a cabin they lived in during the summer in Henderson, North Carolina.

We'd jet-ski and fish from a dock and some people would swing from a rope swing and I'd be too afraid to swing from the rope swing and one time my grandpa took my sister and me into town and we were in this mall and he saw an airplane that was giant and it was made out of foam and would glide for a hundred yards and I saw another airplane that was plastic that you'd shoot like a gun and he said, "Keegan, how 'bout I get this giant foam airplane?" Only I was a crappy whiney kid who whined about everything and I said, "But I want this airplane, WHINE WHINE WHINE."

"Alright," he said. "Let's get both."

In those days he still chewed Red Man chewing tobacco and there were red solo cups everywhere. In his car and on the deck railing and down in the boathouse on the dock where they kept the boat and jet ski and fishing poles. He took out his pouch of tobacco, which had indented a medium-sized rectangle in all of his shirt pockets, and unwrapped it and then grabbed a handful and stuffed it in his mouth and said "KWEEGAUN donnnnawnt dooo this. Gwaaattt me?"

"Yeah, Grandpa. I got you," I said and then he wrapped the pouch back up and put it into his shirt pocket. He grabbed his reading glasses, which may have been on the table or the deck banister railing or somewhere around the deck but they were always near him because he was always reading newspapers and history books, and he opened his airplane box and looked for the instructions. I tore into my box and a few seconds later was shooting my airplane and it was great. It went about five yards or so this way and then I'd chase it and shoot it ten yards or so that way into the forest on the out-skirts of their cabin.

The forest was humid and lush and filled with dirt paths and I'd shoot my plane gun at trees and then chase after it again and sometimes my little sister would raise her hands and get all excited. She was all of three or four years old at the time with beautiful blue eyes and bleached blonde hair kissed by the California sun, and she was always smiling and was always giggling and I looked back up at the deck and my grandpa was reading the instructions, which is what he always did.

I shot my gun plane some more and chased it some more. My sister kept giggling because that's what she did. I didn't know where my parents were. My grandma was worrying, be-cause that's what she did. *Bill. Bill, don't let the kids get dirty,* she'd say. My grandma didn't like germs. *I'm on it,* Grandpa said, looking at the instructions to his foam plane, chew-ing and spitting into his red cup because that's what he did. We all just did what we do when we are in North Carolina, which is one of the things I miss most about being there.

The day before that, a pack of wild horses ran up to the deck out of nowhere and you could hear them before you could see them. They were like a storm rolling through, like thunder coming out of the woods. And my grandma said, AHHHHHHH, *Bill, what is that?* and he said, *Just some wild horses, honey,* all calm and spitting into his cup.

But the horses were more than that too.

They were all kinds of colors and spotted and came from families that had to have been around here since the Spanish brought them over and said, *Go be free and populate this continent,* back when people may or may not have called this place India. The horses didn't look one bit sad, not the way horses look in stables or on farms or before and after and during horse races.

"I think they just want some sugar," my grandma said,

because she likes sugar and we always try to bring comfort to others the way we want to be comforted. She disappeared into the house and she came back a few moments later with some sugar cubes. I would have eaten one too, but the last time I ate food we were supposed to feed to animals, I was a few years younger than that and my aunt and I were fishing off the dock near my grandparents' house in Florida and we'd been eating hot dogs that afternoon and she brought some more and they were cut up in thin slices on a plate and I thought, *That's weird,* but then I ate them just the same and they were cold and I felt sick. "Why are you eating that fish food? You're gonna get sick," my aunt said. And I felt sick but I didn't want to say anything because I didn't want to stop fishing with my aunt who had this awesome Spiderman fishing pole for me to use. This whole fishing thing was quickly turning into my favorite thing of all time. So I just held my puke in until I couldn't hold it in anymore and then we stopped fishing because I puked all over my new clothes my mother had just bought to show me off to her parents in.

But not that day. I wasn't gonna eat those sugar cubes because I'd learned my lesson.

My grandfather had his hand flat with a stack of sugar cubes laid out and the wild horses were licking and slobbering all over his hands because they loved the sugar and my grandma said, "Bill, on second thought maybe this isn't a good idea. Think of the germs," but my grandma was always worried about germs and my grandpa said, "Ahh, don't worry 'bout it," because he never worried about it and he said, "Keegan, come over here," and then put a sugar cube in my hand and I thought real hard about licking it, but I didn't. I was scared to death of puking all over myself again. He lifted me up, up, up, up, up onto his shoulders, "Now keep your hand flat, I don't want you to lose any fingers. Your mom would kill me if you lost a finger," he said, and so I made my hands real flat like a pancake and I tried to stop daydreaming about licking the sugar cube and focused hard on not losing any fingers to these beautiful, wild horses of Spanish descent and my grandma said, "Oh, noooo, Bill, I can't look," and my grandpa was just his quiet self, the way I've always needed him to be.

And then it was just me sitting on his shoulders feeding the horses cubes of sugar. The horses came back a few times that summer and my mom fed them carrots. "I don't want these horses getting fat," my mom said, 'cause she was always worried about someone getting fat, and I never swung from the rope swing into the lake that summer because I was still afraid of dying and so there were things we were learning about ourselves out in those woods.

I kept shooting my airplane at things.

After about twenty minutes of shooting at the trees and plants and the house and the grass and my sister and the sky, the spring broke. *Snap*. Then the plane went *thud* crashing down into the earth and then the gun stopped working.

And so I did what I did back then. I whined.

"Okay, Keegan, I'll fix it for you," Grandpa said.

And he did. But then he finished his plane and I realized how much my plane sucked. And did it ever suck. He threw his off the porch toward the meadow adjacent to the beginning of the woods. It went *UP UP UP UP* and then it leveled off like a real plane and it kept going and going and going. I chased after it and brought it back to him. It felt like his plane hung in the air for ten minutes. He threw it again, and I ran under it, and kept following beneath it as it hung in the sky above my head. I brought it back to him and with a huge bulge of tobacco in his cheek, juices falling into the crevice of his dimple, he said, "Keegan, wanna put a stripe on it?"

Did I ever. "Yeah, Grandpa!"

He leaned over the side of the wooden railing and spit into one of his red cups and grabbed a clear plastic package that had stickers and he let me put a striped sticker on it.

"You want to try throwing this thing," he said.

"Yeah, Grandpa."

And so I did. I threw it up and off the back deck and it didn't go as far as when my grandpa threw it, but it still went way further than my gun airplane flew. Here my grandpa was, sharing his awesome airplane with me, after I whined until he broke down and bought me an airplane that sucked. And he knew my airplane would suck. He lets people make mistakes, which I will always love him for.

I felt a little worse each time I brought the plane back to the deck.

"Want to throw it again?" he said.

"No, I want you to throw it," I said.

"Alright," he said all nonchalant as if he didn't even care that he was throwing the coolest plane ever, which I'm sure he did care about. But that was him. Nonchalant. Cool as a cucumber.

We went like that for a little while and I never said I was sorry. I never said I was sorry for whining, and for missing birthdays and not making more of an effort to see him and Grandma. And I never said sorry for not listening better and for being judgmental and dumb. And I never said sorry for not going to the University of Miami. And I never said sorry for calling the institution of higher education mentioned in the previous sentence the University of Miami and not *The U*. And I never said I was sorry for not telling him how much I loved R&B music and jazz and fishing, and how the two summers I spent in North Carolina were some of my favorite. I never said sorry that my mom and dad changed my name when I was three when they got married from Matthew Keegan Rice to Keegan Matthew Lester. And I never said sorry or thank you all the times I thought I had something figured out and I didn't and he was kind and gracious and quiet with me.

Sorry, Grandpa.

．．．．．．．．．．．．

Outside our car, the trees look like they're dressed up for a shotgun wedding. Spanish moss drips from the branches. Egrets are flying up and up and out from the high grasses shouldering the highway. I think of turning to my dad in the car to tell him all this, about the trees and Grandpa, about naming things and the horses that visited us that summer. But I know if I say all of this, or any of this, he'll just look at me as if I'm an idiot. So I say nothing and instead watch all the trees and swamps and birds the whole way back to the airport.

tour diary: charleston show

....

The Charleston show was good.

Normally doing a show in Charleston, West Virginia, means at least one person leaves having bled, two people have thrown up, and the rest of us, still able to stand, have gathered for a group photo in front of the state's capitol building, which is this huge dome of a building, that sparkles like pirate treasure and looks like someone accidentally left the US Capitol Building in the middle of southern West Virginia.

But not this time.

Everything was good this time. The show was good. Darrin was good. So good I said out loud, *Dang. Darrin's so freaking good tonight,* and someone nudged me—but Darrin looked at me in the eye from the stage as he sang as if to say, *It's alright, li'l buddy.*

Sophia was good too. Her songs were just as familiar and mysterious as ever, like looking at fireworks when you aren't supposed to be moved anymore because you've seen them so many times, and yet you still find yourself losing your breath in their magic.

Howard was good too. When he blacks out on stage, due to his fear of speaking in front of crowds, his patterned button-ups charm and inspire confidence—he's like our tour siren, capable of steering us into the rocks with his beauty and voice and charm.

Kevin was good too. That night he invented a new genre of poetry, *guns and grandmas*, making my knees wobbly every time he spoke.

Bryan was good. He was the most coherent person there, our North Star in the dark who would always lead us home.

Adam was good. He read in his quiet deadpan serial-killer voice and punned a bunch before disappearing. He was so good he went out on a thirty-minute date after the show and said, *Thirty Minutes is all I needed to feel deep shame. Easy peasy.*

John was good. Before I met John R. Miller, I wasn't sure, but now I know that magic exists in the world.

Tyler was real good too. He's like our dad in that he wears dad hats and tells dad jokes and listens to dad rock, and if you ever need one, he'll give you a hug. He makes sure we get to where we're going safe too. And like a dad, he does not want to pull over the tour van for nothing, unless we ask real cute.

ON THE first day of this tour we came up with this phrase: *Pulling a t.* There are various accounts regarding where and how this terminology originated, but I'd like to think it came from someone saying, *I need to tinkle.*

It seems very us.

And of course when in a van that sits twelve people, at least one of us has to *pull a t* all the time. Statistically speaking, at least six people reading this sentence have to *pull a t* right this very second.

We pulled a ton of t's on tour.

As Tyler was driving us home, telling us his dad jokes, and we were singing Bob Seger songs, all of us laughing after this good show in Charleston, West Virginia, where everyone was really good and no one was killed or maimed, someone yelled, *Tyler, I have to pull a t.*

And a few minutes later we were all piling out of the tour van: Tyler, Howard, Sophia, Bryan, Kevin, Darin, Adam, John,

Hannah, and me. We walked out into this field in the middle of Nowhere, West Virginia, and there were stars all above us and all around us and stars as far as we could see, and fifty yards in front of us was a tree line full of fireflies, making the trees shimmer, and we all got into a long line and looked up at the stars above our heads and into the glowing trees and *pulled a t* together in a line, like one giant, tiny sized bladdered family, careful not to cross streams, as we became the thing shimmering in the night.

sometimes my sister is too good at giving christmas presents

....

It all began at dinner, Christmas Eve, when we decided as a family we should just open up all the Christmas gifts under the tree early. Or maybe it started at dinner when someone said, "Joe, how does it feel turning sixty tomorrow?" and my dad said, "Uh, everything hurts, but it's whatever."

It was the first time I'd ever heard my dad sound really sad about anything on his birthday.

AFTER OPENING the presents up, wrapping paper painted the carpet. Bows and cards were everywhere. There was still one last present. There had been big boxes and little boxes and medium-sized boxes, some of which were for one of the three tiny breeds of dogs running around my parents' living room just losing it over the boxes and wrapping paper. They were running circles with boxes on their heads and bows stuck to their bodies and pooping in the slippers left out at the front door. It was pandemonium. But in the middle of all that, there's one unopened envelope left under the Christmas tree.

"Got one more for you, Dad," my sister said, all wily like a fox, pointing at the envelope in the tree, like she knew she just won Christmas. I think that year I wrote a really solid poem for my dad's birthday and Christmas present. I thought, *Holy crap, what else could she get him?* She got him a watch and sunglasses and a robe and a wooden crate with a miniature crowbar for pulling miniature nails out of it, which opened up to a bag of beef jerky. And she got him a beer-making kit and concert tickets. And who knows what else.

He opened up the envelope a little sloppy, his half-drunk scotch sitting on the coffee table, and said, "Oh."

But not in an excited OOOOO and *AHHHHH* way. More in a *I'm a character in a Lifetime movie who just found out my wife is trying to kill me* kind of way.

"Wow, airplane lessons," he said. "Are you trying to kill me?" he said.

I thought he was joking.

This was the first time my dad said anything that acknowledged he could die. Just that past spring my father went to Coachella for the first time. When he got back home, he was badly sunburned and tired. He was tired the way a person who's been to war looks tired. His large frame was hunched over and he didn't resemble my father. My dad, Big Joe, at the age of fifty-nine was finally slowing down. He kept muttering over and over the words *kids* and *dust* and *molly*.

"Are you trying to kill me? Are you trying to kill me? Are you trying to kill me?" he kept repeating to my sister, no matter how hard it made her cry.

IT DEPENDS on who you talk to, but in my opinion, much of the whole fiasco started there.

A few days later we are driving from a town in the desert near Palm Springs to Huntington Beach where he lives. Where I grew up. Out of nowhere my dad says, "Son," which is weird because he never talks to me about nothing.

This must be serious, I think.

My father waits a moment, the way one does before one says something really important. He put his hand to his face, scratching the barely whiskers on his chin. It's obvious the gravity of my response to whatever he's about to ask will be critical. My father is not one for pauses. He's not one for pacing and he's so impulsive that I've heard every idea he's ever had when I've been within earshot. He's the complete opposite of a person who pauses before he talks.

I think, *This must be really serious*. I think, *Cancer*. I think, *His business is going under*. I think, *My parents are splitting up*. *Oh shit*, I think.

And I look at him, but what I see is the sun setting behind him. I see the sun setting over the hundreds of wind turbines jetting up from the California desert. I see the sun setting over the mountains of Idyllwild, over the cars scooting forward in front of us. The setting sun is melting everything into a river of tinsel and red head and taillight, as everything turns to night.

"Something is missing from my life," he says. "Son, I want to sail. I want to sail the Caribbean Blue."

I think he must be joking. Did he just say, *Sail the Caribbean Blue*?

"Oh, okay, Dad," I say.

As we drive on toward Huntington Beach, toward the glinting of its suburban jaws, I think, *This whole sailing the Caribbean Blue thing must be just a thought my father is having*.

"Let's Skype the guy with the boat so you can meet him."

"Meet who?"

"My friend. The Captain."

And I should have said something right there, but like an idiot, I said nothing. I'm always wrong about my father's ambition, especially when it comes to sailing the Caribbean Blue.

....

"Man, we have shit reception down here" are the first words I hear from the captain.

"Yeah, I bet. 'Cause it's Panama," my dad says.

I keep looking out the window as mountains of sand start turning into housing tracts and businesses and later a wall so we can't see all the lives happening on the other side of the highway. The captain is slurring his words and sounding a little too excited, like a salesman. Like a car salesman trying to sell me something. The call ends a while later with my father turning to me and saying, "Panama. So we'd start in Panama." For a second I wonder who the *we* is.

Ah, shit, he means me. Shit. Shit. Shit.

And so I learned that night that my father was not kidding about sailing the Caribbean Blue.

As we pull into our garage, the familiar breeze rolls in from the ocean. It's one of the things I most love about this place. The smell and taste of ocean.

My father grabs a Coors out of the fridge. He plops down on the sofa. He turns on the television.

"Hey, let's call the guy back and see what he's up to."

They Skype for an hour. My dad has never had a conversation with me that lasted longer than eight minutes. The captain talks about how *kick ass* Panama is and sailboats and women and food and guitars he owns and the guitars he wants to buy and how it's all so *kick ass*, and in my head I start to think, *This guy sounds like an asshole.*

Of course when I look at my father, sitting on the couch in a house in suburbia, all by himself in front of his TV, a Coors resting on his stomach, I also recognize the excitement in his face that hasn't existed in years. I haven't seen him excited for

nothing except college football in years, except this one time
when he was convinced there were little red lobster-looking
crab things in the Long Beach harbor.

....

And none of us, not my mom or my sister or me, wanted to go see them, but then that Sunday happened to be Father's Day and so we all said, *Okay, Dad, we'll let you take us to Long Beach so you can show us your crab lobster things.* And you know what? After driving in circles for hours and hours around public docks and private docks and docks for loading great big ships and docks that were more piers for small inflatable boats and cement boat launches and boat launches with no piers that were just gravel walkways, there were no crab things in the water anywhere. And he felt bad. I could see it on his face and in the way he slumped his shoulders. He just wanted to share this thing with us that he was really excited about. And we were walking around some more docks not seeing any of these crab things and my dad was like, *Sorry, guys, I'm so sorry,* and we were like, *Nah, Dad, you're all good,* and he was like, *I don't trust you guys,* and we were like, *No, Dad, it's really okay.* And he got sad, but there was this taco joint nearby and it was going crazy because Mexico was beating the heck out of the USA in a World Cup qualifier and so many people were so happy in a language where I understood some things but not everything. People started cheering and dancing and they came out of the restaurant to hug each other and continued dancing and yelling in a beautiful language. I'll never forget that. That happiness and joy is one of my favorite things my dad has accidentally showed me.

....

And my dad's wearing that kind of lobster-crab thing excitement on his face right now and so I don't say anything about any of it. I don't say, "Dad, your friend sounds like a jerk," which I should have said. In that moment, I should have said, "Dad, your friend sounds like a jerk and we're not going to Panama."

But his eyes were all happy and kind of sparkly and so instead I said, "Well, that sounds like fun," hoping this would be like one of the other ideas he's talked about in the past.

My mother will convince him not to go. She's good at that. She's a boss at that. I'd go as far as saying she's like the Steve Jobs of that, a true visionary.

So I don't worry.

He'll likely lose interest by football season, I keep telling myself. I start praying football season starts in the nick of time and my dad is laid up on the couch with a Coors, saying things like, "You know, we should really try training across Asia. You know just hopping rails all across Asia," during a commercial break between something state versus something tech.

That night I sleep well. But before that, I hear his television still on clear down the hall in his bedroom. His bedroom door's not quite shut. Between my father's rumbling snores, the anchors on CNN talk smugly about Hillary Clinton as the Democratic front-runner and the impossibility of Donald Trump making it out of the primaries, and I hope my dad's dreaming of Panama. I hope he's dreaming ocean and Panama and that both unravel in his dreams. I hope that with each of his deep breaths, the idea of sailing the Caribbean Blue leaves him.

tour diary: lewisburg

....

Today on tour we drove up into Lewisburg. Lewisburg is this small fancy town in southern West Virginia that looks like the European countryside in the kind of movies where people might talk about villas and vineyards and cappuccinos and bike racing. *How fancy is this tiny town? you ask*, Six-dollars-for-a-lackluster-taco fancy. And here we are in our tour van, smelling like we've been in a tour van and like we'd been up all night, which we had been, when we came upon this giant animal.

The giant-looking animal was black with white spots. Tyler slows the van down so we can get a better view and after closer examination, the giant animal in question is a poodle. And this giant cow-looking poodle is doing the waddle animals do when they have to crap, and sure enough the giant cow-poodle waddled a little more before making a circle and popping a squat.

The van erupts in cheering. It started with a, *Hey, guys,* and then a slow clap and then a full-on van cheer as the poodle started crapping. We just got louder and louder and then the poodle went again and we just started clapping and hollering like the cow-poodle animal had just won the Olympics. Bryan had a tear in his eye. And then the cow-looking poodle just walked off into another yard like it was nothing and I wonder how many animals and people go through their entire day with a van full of people cheering for them without their knowing it.

I know what it's like to be the poodle that doesn't know anyone's cheering for it. So if you get a chance, tell the people and animals that make you stand up and cheer, that make you feel things in your body, that move you, tell them they move you. There's nothing harder than going through life thinking you've never moved anyone, or never knowing how loved you really are.

tour diary in the south: putting more heart
in our heartbreak

....

Howard decided a few days before in Huntington, West
Virginia to come to Lexington, Kentucky, with us to hang out
with our friend Joe. And no one went to that reading. People
ended up being in the bar in Lexington as we read because
it was a bar, which is one of the reasons I always try to book
readings in bars.

At the end of the night a man gave us a couple hundred
dollars and bought my book and Adam's zine and wanted to
buy Joe's book, but Joe told him, "Go get it on Amazon. It'll
be cheaper that way!"

And the man did.

"I train racehorses," the man told us.

When you set out to do a book tour, you never plan on
meeting a horse trainer or a writer promoting Amazon. That
night we met both.

After the reading, Howard drove us back from the bar
to Joe's house and it started pouring the rain. All kinds of
lightning was stitching the sky and Howard turned his truck
off in the gravel driveway and played some John R. Miller
as the rain filled Howard's truck bed like a water glass and
it felt like home.

We listened to John cover John Prine covering Blaze Foley's
"Clay Pigeons," and every time I heard the word *Texas*, I
missed my girlfriend. That's where her family came from.

What no one ever tells you about touring is that when you get heartsick and homesick, everyone has something that reminds them of their humanity. There's something that can save your life, that can remind you of who you are. Sometimes it's a song. Sometimes a smell or taste. For me, it's the rain.

WE WENT into Joe's house and sat on the kitchen floor, drinking bourbon from plastic cups, and Adam read his stories to us and the rain smell creeped in through an open window like a friendly ghost. Every so often the night lit up and I knew at any moment the black paint of sky could open, could unzip, and all the light in the world could seep out as if from a wounded mountain.

"I've always wanted to go to Knoxville," Howard said.

So the next day Howard drove us from Lexington, Kentucky, all the way to Knoxville, Tennessee, to this honky-tonk. Adam and Joe and Joe's wife, Molly, were there too.

Doing a reading in a honky-tonk was my idea. I figured everyone loves karaoke. This is gonna be great.

And I didn't know you could smoke in bars in Tennessee. You shouldn't, but there you could. We met some beautiful people that night who smelled like cigarettes and pizza, and the woman who ran the honky-tonk had long white flowing hair and her eyes looked like they had seen some things. She was kind and kept handing us free pizzas. I guess that's what you do for weary travelers in Knoxville.

No one else showed up to this reading either except for Adam's best friend, who drove from Nashville, and a photographer from North Carolina who I'd always wanted to meet. We hugged and I dedicated all my poems to them that night. They told me about driving three hours to get there and then we all left after the show, our bodies and throats too broken from the generations of cigarette smoke to sing karaoke.

We ended up at a huge house party, full of poets, none of whom came to our reading and at some point, sad and buzzed, Adam sat down in the middle of the living room and said, "I want to read one of my stories."

His stories are so good. And he's really good at making jokes while he reads them. And in the middle of the giant poetry party we were at, in some stranger's house in Knoxville, Tennessee, right as he was going to sit down and read a story in front of a room, which he thought was filled with his friends, which reading stories for his friends is for him what the rain and lightning in the sky is for me, a white woman yells out, "The last thing we need is another white male like you reading your poetry at this party."

....

I know Adam must have been thinking about it the rest of the night and all day the next day as we picked up our rental car and drove through Tennessee and into Asheville, North Carolina. I'm sure he must have been thinking about it as we were sitting in a coffee shop drinking overpriced green juice, because we needed greens, because if we ate any more pizza or any more chicken wings or diner food or drank another drop of liquor we'd have died. I'm sure he was thinking about it as we drove all night to Wilmington and maybe even dreamed about it on the couch at Isabelle's house. I'm sure he thought about it today, which is our first day off in a week.

WE STARTED out in Morgantown, West Virginia, where it was winter and then we turned northwest toward Ohio, where it was almost winter, and drove all the way south to Tennessee, and now on a beach in Wilmington, North Carolina, it's not winter.

We were driving Isabelle's car around Wilmington until we found a restaurant on a beach and sat down at a high bar table and watched the Atlantic roll back and forth a while in silence. As we waited on our food, Adam said, "I'm not even white. And I'm not a poet. I'm a writer."

And he's right. So I told him so.

"You're just nice to me when we're drinking," he said.

And we were drinking then, so I didn't know what to say.

"I try to be nice to you all the time," I said.

"If I called myself a Persian writer, people would publish and buy my book, but I don't want to be a Persian writer. I want to be Adam. I want to be a writer. I want to write about people. I want to be the writer Adam," he said behind his Miller heavy can.

AND I was in the same place last year. How does anyone convince someone who can't be convinced of how close they are to accomplishing a goal? No matter how close you are, no matter what anyone says, in your head it still feels like there is an ocean between you and your goal. I'd been ready to give up. I was about to move back home and quit writing for good. Maybe a week or so away from it and then I got my break. There's no difference to me between writers who've published a book and a writer who has finished writing one but hasn't published. They are still writers. They are still people struggling every day. The only difference is how the outside world perceives you.

All I said to Adam was "I know."

I wished I had the language to tell him all of this.

On our way back to Isabelle's house we stopped streaming John Prine for a moment and I realized I was about out of data. We decided to check out Isabelle's CD collection.

"She has two CDs. *Rumors* by Fleetwood Mac and some Father John Misty CD," I said.

"Screw that hipster," Adam said.

No pun about it. It was the most rock-and-roll thing I'd ever heard him say.

At the time I wasn't quite sure which CD he was talking about.

....

That's how it all started. That's how we began touring the entire Deep South with only one CD. And while *Rumors* is arguably one of the greatest albums of all time, listening to it for six hours a day, every day for ten days straight is no good for one's mental health or heart.

"Dreams" was playing just outside of Athens, Georgia, when we blew our tire a couple hours before a reading we were already late for. A nice construction worker helped us change our tire and told us *I love art, man* and *My wife is an art teacher*, and he was wearing skinny jeans and a hard hat so I knew he meant it. He even bought two of my books. *Would you sign them for me?* And I did. I sold more books to him than I did at the reading in Athens.

"Go Your Own Way" was playing as we were at a standstill in Atlanta traffic. We were late for our reading in Chattanooga, Tennessee. Because the car was filled with writers, there was a ton of worrying going on. No one warned us about Atlanta traffic. No one told us you should always add two hours to anywhere you are driving if you have to drive through Atlanta. We crisscrossed that highway three more times over the next ten days. A few weeks later, the bridge we'd driven over several times caught fire and collapsed.

"Let's change this CD," Isabelle said, trying to break the tension.

"As long as it's not Father John Misty," Adam said.

So we streamed some more John Prine and Lana Del Rey and ran out of data.

We were late getting to the venue and changed into our show clothes in the parking lot and walked in during the middle of our reading, but then by some miracle we killed it. It was a great reading and I sold enough books for gas money and the woman who put it on said, *I have a cold but I got you all a hotel room*, and that was the first time in weeks I'd slept on a real bed. We got invited to multiple parties but instead we went to a diner, ate dinner around midnight, and then went to sleep. It was the most glorious sleep of my life. The next morning Adam and I walked around Chattanooga and looked at a train depot and paid too much money for green juice while Isabelle met up with a friend, fell in love with the city, and vowed to return someday. Then we hopped back into the car.

AT THAT point we'd been listening to a ton of *Rumors*. Adam always started the session by saying, "Whoa, easy there. Nothing but the hits now."

Most of our conversations were about *Rumors* or being late.

Isabelle would say something about something from the album and then giggle a little like she was about to break into a million pieces of scattered porcelain because that's how she jokes.

And I would just say a lyric with no hint of sarcasm in my voice trying to show the absurdity of it all, because that's how I joke.

And Adam, he'd just pun on lyrics from the album because that's how he jokes.

We didn't know it yet, but we were all heartbroken because you can't listen to that much *Rumors* and not be heartbroken.

Isabelle missed her boyfriend and her dog back in Wilmington, and I missed my girlfriend back in New York, and Adam missed this girl he saw in a parking lot as we stopped to get tacos before our reading in Nashville, Tennessee. We were all so heartbroken.

"THE CHAIN" was playing when we were on the highway that takes you up above the water and marshlands and bayou into New Orleans. None of us had been to New Orleans and we were all excited about having a day off. We'd left the sandy streets of Wilmington, for Athens, Chattanooga, Nashville, and Tuscaloosa and were looking forward to not having to drive for six hours anywhere tomorrow and most especially not having to listen to *Rumors*.

Andrew, my friend from the internet, had a beautiful gigantic one-bedroom apartment just outside the French Quarter. We squeezed our way between two houses and then into a backyard full of sculptures and wild trees and flowers to a rickety staircase. It looked like an old man, twirling up fifteen feet into the sky above New Orleans. Every time we went up and down the stairs, the wood made a sound that sounded like *don't step too hard I might crumble at any moment.*

And that's another thing no one tells you about tour is that at any moment you can die. There're just so many ways to die on tour.

We were all very aware of it at that point, especially after listening to *Rumors* as much as we were. All we could think about was dying and heartbreak and dying from heartbreak.

So when Andrew saw us, he must have thought we were crazy.

I'd been on the road for six weeks and Adam had been for two weeks, and we'd just added another show in Akron, Ohio, which meant we'd be out another three weeks.

Isabelle was ready to kill us and she'd only been out with us six days plus a couple in Wilmington.

Adam was hoping she would kill us.

Andrew was calm as could be though. He whipped up a vegan soup, which was perhaps the only thing vegan that had touched our lips in days.

We started to feel like humans again.

THE READING in New Orleans was great. It took place in an old hotel in a gorgeous ballroom and a bunch of people came out for it. The hotel was so gorgeous that I thought, *This hotel must be haunted.*

Two trans writers read and they stole the show. They were hilarious and sweet. And I was like, *Shit, I have to go on after them.* My friend Andrew from the internet was really good too. He read love poems that did their best to mend our broken hearts. And I was like, *Shit, I have to go on after him.* A friend of mine from West Virginia read, and she was good too, yelling political messages that riled up the crowd and got people in the crowd to believe. Isabelle was really good, and made me think, *One day she's going to be the poet laureate of the United States.* So I went and grabbed myself a drink. Adam was good at his usual deadpan self as he introduced us, punning the entire time.

"Players only love you when they're playing," he said, "like this next poet. But I'm afraid it's Miller time, so I'm gonna grab a beer from back that way, as the next reader needs no introduction," which meant it was my turn to walk up. And so I walked up and yelled poems at the innocent bystanders about my grandma and orcas, and Adam grabbed himself a Miller heavy.

THIS WASN'T like other tours where we were in a van and someone else drove us and someone else made sure we had a place to stay and someone else made sure we were fed and someone else sold merch and someone else was good at talking to unruly people who didn't want to pay us and someone else was good at talking to us and giving us a hug when we needed it, and all we were responsible for was performing. During this tour, we had to drive and perform and document it and I had to make sure we had a place to sleep every night and that at least one person knew we were coming to their town, mostly so we had a place to stay. We divided driving into days beforehand so we knew who could drink and who could not drink. And if we weren't driving that day, we'd sit in the back seat holding a cocktail focusing as hard as we could, pretending we were not sitting in the back seat of a car and pretending that we were not heartbroken for the six hours of road we had ahead of us. All the while Fleetwood Mac would do their damnedest to convince us otherwise.

The New Orleans reading was the week after Mardi Gras, so everyone in town was as dead on the inside as we were. We didn't have to drive anywhere the next day and were a little broken, partially from the tour and partially from the Fleetwood Mac album *Rumors*, and so maybe we drank a little harder than we should have before the reading and at the reading and after the reading.

After our great reading we ended up with our new friends from the reading in a diner that also served drinks, and we had some diner food to go with our drinks. Then we were invited back to the house of two of the readers because they weren't old enough to go to the bars.

And I don't know if it was drinking too much, which it probably was, or maybe listening too much to John Prine and *Rumors*, which it was that too, or if it was just that I really missed my girlfriend, which I did, but in Andrew from the internet's truck, on the way to the third location, I started crying and I couldn't stop.

I missed my girlfriend who was back in New York City and so I called her and said, "I miss you, bear," which is what I call her.

"You sound drunk," she said.

This is getting off to a bad start I thought. So I said, "I'm not that drunk."

And then she let me have it. She let me have it for how I never called her enough and how she didn't like the company I was keeping and that it was too much, and she let me continue to have it after Andrew from the internet parked his truck and turned off his truck's engine at the house party. And she let me continue to have it as we got to the apartment as I walked up some creaky wooden steps that were pretty sturdy considering what we'd become accustomed to, and she continued to let me have it. So I just sat out on the deck as everyone else went into the party and I listened to the most beautiful voice in the whole wide world let me have it for thirty or so more odd minutes until Isabelle came out and said, "Are you coming in? Why are you crying? Are you on the phone still? Jesus fucking Christ."

And she took the phone and said, "No one in their right mind wants to be away from their loved ones this long. He's not doing this to hurt you. Leave him alone. He won't stop crying, damn it." And then she handed me the phone and walked back into the party.

Isabelle had decided to become our manager a few days back and had taken the role very seriously. She started promoting for us and asking people things for us and I was both grateful and terrified. Poet laureate might be too low of a bar. I realized she could do anything in this life that she wanted.

And then the tone on the other end of the phone changed. My girlfriend in her new tone said, "I'm sorry."

And I said, "I just want to come home."

And she said, "I'm sorry," and I said, "I just want to come home," and she said, "I'm sorry."

AND I couldn't go home, so I went into the house full of young writers, who were all beautiful and young and smoking packs of cigarettes as if the link between cigarettes and cancer was still unknown. And Adam was in a room with one of the girls talking about her BoJack Horseman poster. I grabbed some water and tried to calm down a bit.

After a while, Isabelle said, "Time to go," in her manager tone that she'd gotten really good at.

So I picked myself up and threw back the entire cup of water like it was a shot and we went looking for Adam. Adam was still in the bedroom, but now he was in the closet. Not with the girl. Just by himself. And he had the door shut.

"This is my home now. I don't want to leave."

"Okay, Adam," I said. I was gonna let him stay. I know how that feels. Plus we have a day off tomorrow.

"You can't stay in a stranger's closet, Adam," Isabelle said.

"WHY NOT?" Adam groaned.

And by and by, Adam came out of the closet and we went to another bar and got a drink and went home to Andrew's.

THE NEXT day Isabelle wondered if we were going to do group things and then suggested that we all go our own way. So we went our own way.

Isabelle must have really scared my girlfriend because the whole day I got messages from people saying, *I love you* or *Keep going* or *You're living the dream.*

My girlfriend told all my friends to text or call me. And they did. And so as I walked around looking at all the beautiful balconies and roads and homeless people of New Orleans, my pocket pinged every few minutes because people were telling me "I love you" and "Keep going." It even started to rain for a few minutes.

ADAM AND I met up later on. We couldn't stop thinking about tomorrow because yesterday was gone and thus decided this was a good day to take off from drinking.

We each drank only one of those Styrofoam daiquiris and the sugar alone was enough to schedule a doctor appointment to see if we'd contracted diabetes.

"That's not how you get diabetes," Adam said after I made the diabetes joke.

Then we went to the House of Blues for happy hour and ate and had a drink each. Then we went and looked at the Mississippi River, which looked about what you'd think the Mississippi River might look like: a wide river with a muddy mouth that can kill you if you're not careful. And after looking for a while into the jaws of a river that could kill us, we got cold.

So we walked back into town, had another drink, and walked back home to Andrew's.

When we got there, Andrew and Isabelle were sitting out on the porch balcony on the second story. The steps creaked *be careful how you step on me* with each step we took, so we were extra careful.

The porch overlooked the French Quarter and a backyard full of sculptures and art and palm trees and banana trees. The sun made its slow descent and everything looked beautiful like a postcard. And for a moment nothing hurt.

Quiet, the four of us sat, looking out over all of it while the sun curled into itself.

Then the stars popped out and were twinkling above our heads and for a moment none of us wanted to kill the other. And none of us were thinking about the Fleetwood Mac album *Rumors* or our breaking hearts or of wanting to be somewhere else.

Andrew from the internet started talking about flying airplanes and being a teacher and the things people do to each other sometimes. And beneath those stars popping in the night sky, Isabelle and Adam and I became Andrew's students. His children. His biggest fans. We were so happy just sitting on his balcony listening to him because we knew tomorrow we would have to leave and that in Tallahassee, Florida, we would have to be writers again, when all we wanted was to stay there on that porch looking up at the stars, listening to the person who'd let us be his children.

there were also readings

....

like the one in Cambridge where I read with a bunch of Harvard students on the second floor of a café next to Harvard and it looked like a giant octagon cage. I felt a little like a dumb version of Matt Damon in the movie *Good Will Hunting* and I wanted to yell, "How do you like them apples?" but everyone was so nice that I just yelled my poems instead. My cousin was there and she drove three hours from Vermont through a snowstorm. I don't get to see her much because she doesn't live in West Virginia anymore. I read a poem about her dad, and I couldn't see her while I was doing it but people told me she was crying through the whole thing. And after the reading we just got to stand around and talk and be cousins and when she whispered in my ear it was undeniable that it was the voice of my family.

And there was the reading I did in Provincetown, twelve hours after getting food poisoning. It was my first time to Cape Cod and it was so beautiful there. Even though I was so sick that I thought I was going to die, I did the reading and my girlfriend got to go and we stayed in an old house in a room that had a low triangle ceiling so you had to watch out so you wouldn't hit your head. You could hear a church bell tolling down the way, which we came to find out wasn't a church at all but the library I was reading in that night. The room I was reading in was called the Marc Jacobs reading room and it was more beautiful than a purse. On the second floor sat a large marooned sailboat caught on the shoals of the library. Dogs were running everywhere. And I've never slept so good. And no matter where in Provincetown we went, we ran into people and dogs from the reading.

And there was my first time in Akron where someone told me he drove a whole hour to see me read, and the next time I was in Akron he came again. And even Howard came up from West Virginia for the reading and drove me in his truck to the airport the next day.

That was the last day of tour this year for my first book.

Except two weekends later I got on a train and trained out of New York City and up to the Hudson Valley, which I never even knew existed. I read poems in Rhinebeck, New York, in the most beautiful barn I'd ever seen and that was the end of the tour, until a couple weeks later I read in Dallas, Texas, which was a dream of mine and I learned that people in Texas love buying poetry books. A few hours later I was on a plane to California to read for the first time near the place I was born.

When I walked into the venue, my godfather was there and my dad was there and a few neighbors were there and some strangers I didn't know were there and I drank too much because I was nervous because the only me these people know is the me I buried a decade and a half ago. Before I knew it, the reading was over and I had to go back to being just regular me.

Some days I don't want to have to put my poet costume back on quite yet. Other days I can't wait to meet you and explore your home. I'll keep my suitcase ready to go, just in case, if you promise to leave your front porch light on for me.

graduation

....

One day out of the blue, Francis emailed me asking, *Can you help me with this?*

This ends up being a graduation speech. My friend Franny was chosen to give a speech at his med school graduation. I couldn't be more proud of him.

Until I read his graduation speech.

The speech was terrible. It was stiff in a way that's not Francis at all and after a first read over, I decided: *this graduation speech is shit.*

FRANCIS IS the guy I once shared a cruise ship room with and on this boat there was a club and a beautiful French girl was across the dance floor one night and he just glided across the floor and swooped in and, with the magic of someone from a black-and-white movie, started dancing with this beautiful French girl all across the floor, twirling and dipping. If there'd been a camera, it might have zoomed in on her face and you'd literally see the air in her body escape her. That same night we made friends with a couple of Russian girls who were cousins, who lived in Brighton Beach, and he was just as smooth and charismatic as he was on the dance floor, but different. He's personable in a way foreign to me. Over the years I've been hardened by New York. And that night we discovered a place that served all-you-can-eat chicken wings.

So we ate plate after plate of chicken wings, figuring out the quickest way to eat them, learning that the flats had the most tender meat and then went back every night and ate three or four more plates with our new Russian friends. There was a day where we rented a moped and just rode for hours around an island. After this and watching *The Motorcycle Diaries*, Francis was determined to motorcycle across South America and one day Vietnam and possibly India. Except for the bouts of seasickness he suffered every day and him going on and on about the brilliance of Malcolm Gladwell, the cruise was a smashing success.

When I said over the phone, "Francis, this speech is shit. Let's rewrite your speech," he was quiet for a moment.

"Yeah. I knew it needed work, but . . . I wasn't sure what it needed."

I meant to say, there's nothing in this speech that shows how smooth you are or how good of a dancer you are or how good you are at making friends with random strangers or how good you are at being hip or how much you like eating chicken wings or being Vietnamese, or graduating from our high school, where only 7 percent of students go on to four-year colleges, or motorcycling or jujitsu or about what an idiot Malcolm Gladwell is. There is nothing in this speech that shows what an amazing human you are.

Of course I did not know how to say it over the phone, so I said, "This is terrible. What about Bruce Lee? You still into him?"

"Yeah. Of course."

"What about that quote about water? Write a vignette about that. And then just write funny things you saw during podiatry school and things you saw on YouTube while you were at podiatry school."

"Oh, okay. I got it."

And after a couple more rewrites, he did get it.

It went from a boring graduation speech about feet to a

roast of the entire podiatry class, with a long extended arching metaphor riffing on the Bruce Lee quote about water, and I said, "Are you sure you want to make fun of all these people," and he said "yeah," and I was thankful he wasn't quoting Malcolm Gladwell, so I said, "Awesome! Looks good. I'll come up and teach you how to read it the day of graduation."

"Great. See you next Monday."

SUNDAY NIGHT before his graduation I had two readings. Both were great.

During the first, I stood up and tried to make people laugh. And they laughed. I yelled at people standing around the reading from the stage and then I told them some poetic things, which is just a way to get people to listen to me yell at them in a space where I'll get paid in drinks and admiration.

And they listened.

And my girlfriend said, "That was a great reading."

And then some strangers said, "That was a great reading," and the host said, "Would you hold on a second, for a picture? That was a great reading."

And I said, "Thank you, thank you, thank you, and yes."

This reading was in a tiny bar in a Brooklyn neighborhood called Crown Heights, which is well on its way to being gentrified. The bar makes great drinks though, and the drinks are free, which is my favorite price to pay for a drink and it often makes drinks taste better. And at these things someone always buys me another drink and says, "You were great," and I say, "Thank you," even though I should say, "Thank you, but I'm good."

I like reading in small bars because I like to yell. People say, *How innovative of you to yell at me like that.* And I say, *I learned it from my parents.*

AFTER THE reading, I kiss my girlfriend and say, *I'll see you after the next reading*, which was on the other side of

Brooklyn, in a neighborhood called Bushwick, a neighborhood that's been gentrified for what feels like ten years. This
venue is in an old warehouse converted into a cabaret theater
called the House of Yes and everyone dresses sexy there
except for me, because I know trying to be sexy never works
for me. Yelling is my bread and butter.

So an hour later I get to the venue. I do this reading, which
is more of a show than a reading, which means *fun*, and
there are more free drinks and *you are greats* and me yelling at people about orcas and West Virginia and how much I
love my mother and father and grandma and little sister and
football and stars and the way the moon hangs low when you
most need it, like a perfect wingman.

This theater is filled with hundreds of people and I have
to yell into a microphone or they'd never hear me. After I'm
done yelling at them and telling them about my grandma and
the great work of the moon, people backstage change out of
their sexy clothes into their normal-people clothes and we all
finish our drinks. We say, *You were great, you were great,*
and *you were great too*, and we are all just people again,
which is how I like us best.

I get on the subway and take it an hour and half back to
Morningside Heights, where I pack my bag. I take an hour
nap and then it's four thirty in the morning and I get back
on the subway and head to the Megabus depot and get on a
Megabus and take off to Philadelphia.

All the lights of New York turn into distant stars, then
lakes of darkness. All the towns are sleeping in the dark as
we pass them. Everyone is sleeping now except for the truck-
ers and the gas station attendants, a few cross-eyed lovers,
the insomniacs worrying, our bus driver, and me. The May 9,
2016, *New York Times* headline in my lap reads, "Worried?
You're Not Alone." Another headline reads, "It's Thought
Dinosaurs Once Cooed Like Doves." And I think, *Of course
they did.*

The sun starts pulling its head up as I nod in and out of consciousness. Before I know it, a web of highways and bridges and a skyline are visible, and I might have been a little delirious, but it was one of the most beautiful sunrises I'd ever seen from a Megabus. And I'm sure I looked and smelled like last night—who doesn't on a Megabus? Our fears should never keep us from enjoying a good sunrise, especially on a Megabus.

The bus lets us off in Philadelphia and the sun is up and touching everything.

At first it is soft and enjoyable but then it turns annoying and hot and piercing. I grab a coffee at the Dunkin' Donuts, because no one judges you at Dunkin' Donuts and clearly I'm going to need as much coffee as possible if I'm going to survive this.

Hong, Francis's girlfriend, has been texting with me and gave me an address. I'd recently deleted my Uber app, because deleting it was described to me as the progressive thing to do and nothing is more progressive than following orders and deleting apps. White people protests are always about deleting something.

How does Lyft even work?

After I get Lyft to work, I end up in an apartment that is gorgeous. Though it's a five-story walk-up. Francis and Hong and two of his other friends rented it for the weekend. "Wow, this apartment is beautiful," I say. *Philadelphia is really pretty when one is not stuck in a snow apocalypse*, I think.

"Yeah." Francis says, nervous, with his nervous laugh, which I pick up on this time, like a good friend.

THEY TAKE me to the bedroom, which is fancy and hip and covered in contemporary art with gold-streaked spray paint and deer and a fixie bike, which I imagine was a huge selling point.

"Read the speech to me," I say.

"Alright. DearStudentsfacultyparents,todayweare—"

"Whoa. Slow down."

"Okay."

"Dear Students, faculty, parents, today we are—"

"Better. Make sure to pause after every couple of sentences. And be loud. Speak like you wrote this thing, and that it matters."

Francis nods.

"You want everyone to hear your jokes, so think pacing too. You want the joke about Tyler and his fascination with Justin Bieber and Lacoste and well you want his family to be able to hear it. So be loud and slow."

Francis nods.

"And take a few moments between vignettes. You don't want to confuse people when you jump from Bruce Lee to potential and YouTube. Got it?"

"Got it," he says.

"And you have to really sell Bruce Lee here, so make sure to elaborate on what he meant to you and young Franny Dinh. The Franny Dinh who only knew two sentences of English his first day of school. And what were those two sentences?"

"Hi, my name is Francis. Want to be my friend?"

"Yup and who taught you that?"

"My mom."

"And where will she be today?"

"In the audience."

"Yeah, but where?"

"Uh."

"In the audience of your medical school graduation, that you are delivering the keynote speech to, so you better be loud and slow so she can soak up every moment of it. She taught you your first two sentences of English and now you are giving your medical school graduation speech. And how did that go? The 'Hi, my name is Francis. Want to be my friend?' "

"I got bullied until I went to college."

"Exactly. Beautiful. I bet you and probably every single one of your podiatrist classmates got bullied too. That is going to pull some heartstrings. Don't talk directly into the mic. Slow down. You can never go too slow."

"Got it. Got it."

And I think, *This is gonna be great.*

All the jokes are pretty good. We reworked them a little. He's slowing down, reading smooth like the Francis I know.

WE GET to the auditorium in some stupid Lyft that is super inconvenient and makes us walk out of our way many blocks to find the driver and I am pretty sleepy because I'd only slept three hours in the last day and a half and I am cranky and we open the car door and get out and there's Francis's parents.

"Hi, Keegan," his dad says.

"Hi, Keegan," his younger sister says.

His mother looks at me and has no idea who I am. The last time I saw them, Francis and I were practicing songs in our high school rock band, which we convinced his parents would help us get scholarships, otherwise all rock-and-roll activities would have been out of the question.

"Thank you for helping Francis with his speech," his father says. "I hear you are living in New York City. A writer. Your parents must be proud."

"Thank you. I think they sort of are," I say.

AND BEFORE I know it, Hong and Francis's parents and his sister and I are being ushered into the auditorium down a special aisle toward our seats, in a special section roped off for *The Family of the Graduation Speaker.*

THAT'S US.

The room is real old. I'd been in this kind of room before. It's large and angular and was likely at one point a church and the voice carries naturally. Unfortunately, people suck at preaching these days and need mics and add speakers in places where they should not be, which cuts out all feeling from the preaching. There is something about having to go to another register, to force yourself to be loud so that others can hear you, that gives a kind of credibility to storytelling. Most speaker systems in churches are utter disasters.

I get a little teary-eyed about all of it. I'm so proud of Francis. He's younger than me and finished medical school and is delivering his graduation speech, which seems so far away from us talking about the Decembrists and playing Coldplay covers on his family piano in the living room. It's far away from Huntington Beach, a town the majority of our peers were trapped in. We were far away, living in East Coast cities, becoming the people we thought we were meant to be. We were trying to make dream lives for ourselves because our parents were told they couldn't. Only Francis became a doctor and I got good at yelling at people in bars.

AND LIKE I figured it would, the graduation absolutely sucked. All the professors spoke directly into the mic and mumbled or talked too fast. It was twenty minutes of bass mumbles at a time and then everyone got their names called.

When the person in the funny-looking hat and the Harry Potter robe mumbled *Francis Dinh*, I feel like a parent. He's done it. He's Dr. Dinh now.

Francis once wanted to be in a band. He once wanted to make films about the experiences of hip, first-generation Vietnamese teens growing up and coming of age and probably riding fixies or something. He might have wanted to be a writer once too. When he found out I changed my undergraduate major from political science with an emphasis in Africa and the Middle East to creative writing, we were sitting on his lawn looking up at the moon and he was wearing skinny jeans and a shirt to some band I'd never heard of and he said, "You ever read *The Unbearable Lightness of Being*?"

and I said, "Shut up, you hipster," and then suggested he check out Chang Rae Lee's *Native Speaker*, which was the last book I read.

His family is in the pharmacy business and he has relatives who own chains and chains of pharmacies and we always joked that he would go to school and become a doctor because he had to become a pharmacist to keep the family business going. But he ended up doing that and not doing that because he fell in love with the idea of giving people a second chance at life, which is very him. He found a way to take an idea and turn it into a vocation and then career. He gets to think like Franny the musician and Franny the writer and Franny the person who wanted to make films for young Vietnamese teens to have role models to look up to. He gets to be the next generation of Bruce Lee and he gets to be a builder and a mender of people.

Then it was time for his speech.

People were hanging on to his every word. He spoke slow. People laughed and cried and felt things. Francis's mom cried and his dad cried and Hong said, "He's so good."

And I said, "Yeah. He's great."

AFTER THE graduation people kept coming up and saying, *I had no idea Bruce Lee is so deep. I want to be like water too.* And then everyone started drinking out of Dixie cups and I was drinking coffee because I thought I was about to die and Francis's younger cousin came up and said hi.

"HI, WHERE are you from?" I asked.

"Huntington Beach."

"Whoa, me too." And then I found out we went to the same catholic school.

"Yeah. The kids aren't very nice," he said.

"They weren't nice to me either. What do they say to you?"

"Well, my uncle used to be a priest." He paused for a

moment and looked around like he was about to tell a secret, which could not have been much of a secret if his classmates were already bullying him about it. "But he quit because he fell in love and now he isn't a priest anymore."

"Ah, well don't let them get you down. As soon as you get to college everything changes. Trust me. I was the kid everyone picked on too."

"Wow, really?"

"Yup."

AND THEN his sister pushed him to the ground and ran away and he got himself up and chased after her through the string of podiatrists and their families holding onto their Dixie cups of beer and wine and Styrofoam plates full of prime rib.

I walked over to Francis.

"Hey, man. You never told me that your uncle quit being a priest."

"Yeah. Ha ha."

That was a nervous Francis laugh.

"Wow, after all that."

"Yeah."

"That must be something to get the chance to relearn to love again at that age," I said. I smiled a crooked smile. "I mean, I'm sure God's not pissed at him or nothing. I mean that's the only story that starts with 'my uncle used to be a priest but isn't anymore' that has a happy ending. I mean, it's awesome," I said.

I'm always saying the wrong thing at the wrong time and never quite what I mean.

Francis smiled back at me. He knew that I couldn't help it, but that I love him. "How are your parents doing?" he asked.

"Well, my dad's lost somewhere out in the Caribbean, right now," I said, "which as it turns out is much larger than you'd think. He's in some broken down sailboat with some jerk captain and some other guy, who I don't know anything about. I haven't heard from him in days and my mom and sister have been trying to call the coast guard and authorities off the Panama Coast, which is where he left from. But like sovereignty is more complicated these days than you'd think, so it's been a bit of a struggle figuring out who are the right authorities. Email prayer chains have been started. I'm not sure what's left for me to do. People have been working around the clock trying to locate him. But I'm just, you know, trying to keep myself busy."

....

One of the conversations I had with my father while he was lost at sea made me certain he wasn't praying like Francis's uncle. My dad took a boat, but not to escape oppression or war or hunger. It wasn't like when he left West Virginia in search of work and a life.

"Keegan," he'd said, in a voice that was both my father's and not my father's. He sounded like a stranger. Maybe it was the voice of the person he had been before he was my father. Maybe this was *Bigs*, the name my uncles pinned to him. The stranger's voice sounded tired and worn like an old pair of jeans, possessing both a comfort and the ability to tatter at the seam at any moment. His voice was wrapped in a mechanical chrome. A disguise that may have been his satellite phone or poor reception or the storm that was all around him as he and the two others clamored in their boat that was made to be sailed in a lake, in a place protected by shores and shallow waters, where there were no swells or hurricanes or sharks. Instead, as if flying a prop plane through space, they were bobbing around in a giant unending black pool of Caribbean, hundreds of miles from anything they could step onto, where they'd not sink.

Already, only days into a three-week journey, they'd run out of gas and torn their sail.

"After we ran out of gas, the fridge stopped working because we couldn't use the generator. So we threw most of our food overboard about day three," he said, something smacking in his voice I'd never heard before. Partially fear but more than anything, fatigue. And as long as I've lived, I've never seen or heard my father sound tired. *This must be Bigs*, I thought. "I snuck a bag of beef jerky onto the boat and told no one," he said. "The captain's dog could smell it on me though, so sometimes it would just be me and him, this tiny little pug crapping everywhere beneath deck, with our hidden bag of beef jerky, our only hope. Sometimes I wonder if we'll ever get off this boat."

....

Listening to the podcast I recorded with Francis a few years ago, I hear all the small things happening at once that I couldn't hear then. I can hear the snow and wind more perfectly, the pride in Francis's voice when he says the words *Pray*, *Priest*, and *Vietnam*. I can sense his smile when he says, *I was the first of the Dinh family to be born in America*, when he says, *I'm Catholic*. I hear pride in his voice when he talks about grappling and mixed martial arts and what Bruce Lee means to him as a philosopher, a fighter, and one of the few available versions of Asian masculinity he would see on television or in movies or on a billboard or box of cereal as a young person growing up in the same sleepy beach town in Southern California as me.

We both identified with not belonging to the place. But his want to belong made us different. He'd talked about maybe raising a family there someday and that it wasn't so bad. And now his view on it has changed, because he's lived in other places. Whatever struggle it is we both had with the place, one of the things we can agree on is that neither one of us can separate ourselves from it; nor can we claim that we haven't been shaped in some way by it.

I can hear the fear in Francis's voice at the start of the interview and how, as he moves from feeling like he's being interviewed to telling a story, that fear wanes like a star burning out in the night.

I listen to this interview in the years following, as I crisscross America on buses and planes, when I feel most like a stranger. I listen to him nights when I feel like I don't have a friend in the world. I listen to him when I'm homesick. I listen to him in the familiar food courts of airports on my trek back West. Sometimes I listen to him in New York City, lying in bed at night when everything's real dark, and I can hear the

outside world calling out to me, *Who are you? Who are you?*
Where are you from? Who do you belong too?

I LISTEN to this recording every day while my father is lost at
sea.

part five

the doldrums

....

People contain multitudes. I learned this from my father and from West Virginia. I learned that the closer you get to something you prize, the further from everything else you will find yourself. I learned this in all the faces of my friends whose weddings I've missed, my mother's face each time I say the word *home*, and she knows I don't mean the place I was raised. I've learned it in the rhododendron my aunt gives my grandma each summer. I learned it in the last voicemail my father left me while he was lost and floating aimlessly in the Caribbean, hundreds of miles from the coast of Jamaica, in a place devoid of wind. A place where mountains deadened the breath of the gods, called the doldrums.

My father is lost beneath the same stars that have guided weary searching travelers for centuries. The voice in the voicemail he left me was not my father's though. It was the voice of the stranger he'd become. He said, "If you could see all of this—you'd love it. You'd understand."

Moonlight was filling up the water all around him. He said, *Dolphin*. He said, *Dolphin*. He said, *Dolphin dolphin dolphin*. He said, "Dolphins were jumping up and out of the ocean, from what looked like a beam of moonlight. There were so many dolphins last night, buddy. I'm not sure what it means, but I know it must mean something."

*when my father got lost at sea i started
doing things i normally don't do*

....

For instance: I googled *differences between ocean and sea*.

There aren't many differences.

The main difference is a sea is smaller than an ocean. But, from the data I've crunched, my father has the same chance of drowning in either. A person can drown in a bathtub or a child's inflatable pool. I googled that too. It's happened about eighty-seven times this year.

I started wondering about the geography of Central America and the Caribbean Sea. I started wondering about how sovereignty works and why officials in Nicaragua and the US Coast Guard couldn't work with officials in Panama.

I'm sure some of you are laughing at me.

In that google search I learned that some things are bigger than my father being lost at sea.

Then I started going to the movies. I saw documentaries and historical fictions and comedies and movies that some people call films, because aspects of the movie utilize surreal elements, even though it's unclear whether the director was pretentious or just trying to dream like they could dream when they were a child dreaming in their childhood bed. And somehow even dreaming has become pretentious these days. And yet, I tried to dream the way I once dreamed as a child too, but it was a no-go. I mostly just tossed and turned at night.

I started walking to a church called St. John the Divine. Sometimes in the mornings and sometimes in the afternoons. And sometimes both.

It's not a church as much as it's a cathedral with art installations, and I wasn't really going there to be told comforting things. I just needed a reason to walk out of the apartment because sitting at a table looking out over the Hudson River wondering, *Is my dad alive?* over and over and over is no way to spend your life. I like going to the cathedral when the old man who always wears a cardinal red V-neck sweater cleans the organ pipes. There'd be so much noise that after a while I felt like I was floating. So sometimes I'd go to this cathedral to feel like I was floating.

There are three peacocks living on the grounds of St. John the Divine. I made friends with them and renamed them Darbie and Oreo. I only needed two names because two of the peacocks were colored the same exact way and one was albino and I'm not vain enough to tell you I can tell the difference between the colorful peacocks. I started having lunch with Darbie and then Oreo. They weren't sure of me at first, which I appreciated about them. But after a while, they started warming up to me. I ended up talking a bunch to my friends Oreo and Darbie and they were always patient with me and willing to listen.

Each night, I played basketball in the gym across the street. I'm not very good and fairly short. The first time I played was earlier in the year. I quit watching the NFL a couple years back because I think what's most broken in America is most evident in the NFL. The night of the Super Bowl I went to the gym across the street and to my surprise the basketball courts were full. It was mostly Chinese grad students.

While not a gifted shooter or by any means tall, I learned that night I could still do other things and contribute to a group of people who *could* play basketball. I learned I could be really good. Not at contributing points but at laying screens and using my small body to take charges. This means to use my small body to stop much stronger, much larger, much more athletically gifted Chinese grad students by stepping into their path as they bullet their bodies across the court toward the hoop.

After months of this, I can say with full honesty that even I was starting to show improvement in the way I got run over.

That first night though, I'd run up and down the court with no idea of what people were saying or trying to say to me and it was a strangely quiet game, the way we played it. We didn't need names or words. Our eyes were doing much of that work. It was quiet except for the wind in our footsteps carrying us up and down the court.

Every night since my dad's been lost at sea, I've played basketball because there's something about getting run over by another human that I've begun to crave. I find myself needing that human contact to remember that *yes, I am still alive* and *none of this is a dream.*

ain't, ain't a word

....

and only the hillbillies on The Beverly Hillbillies say y'all, a teacher in California told me in the fourth grade—and it was there I learned that it's wrong to say the thing you feel if the people around you wear nicer clothes than you.

One night my friend said, *When my great papa came over on the boat, he ate a banana whole. Didn't even peel it*, and I said, *Mine did too*, and then I thought: I wonder if this was just another story people tell their children like Santa Claus or was there a great banana shortage?

My girlfriend's father said, *My dad grew up in a Greek village that was still in the Stone Age with no running water or electricity*, and I said, *So did my grandma*, and I thought and so did everyone in my family who ever lived before her too.

I had a professor in grad school tell me, *Don't write the way you speak. The point of writing is to get it perfect.* My grandma always says *not to give a shit about what anyone thinks if you know you're right* and I speak perfect, so I never paid mind to it. It feels unnatural to string together so many bizarre and long-winded words that no one's ever heard before into a sentence. But that's my professor's perfect. Maybe he wishes to speak the way he writes but can't. Why is that my problem?

In grad school someone said not to refer to Catholicism in my writing. He said, *But it's okay to use Greek mythology.*

He told my friend not to use Spanish in her writing so she wrote *puta*.

Academic male writers love to write of the woods and all the things they would kill with their hands in the woods if they'd ever been in the woods. But I don't do that because I've seen so many deer strung up, draining blood into buckets like a leaky faucet, that it's nice to sometimes see them alive.

My uncle had a girlfriend from New Jersey and one time he drove her to a gas station just outside of Morgantown because there was a WVU football game that day and it would be easier to get some beer for the tailgate there, and while they were looking at Michelob Ultra and his girlfriend was talking shit on him for drinking Michelob Ultra, like *What kinda man drinks Michelob Ultra?* and *What kinda man counts calories?* right then two men walked in with rifles over their shoulders and big knives on their hips, wearing camo head to toe, and she said, *Oh shit, I think they are gonna rob the store,* and then the attendant yelled out, *Jerry, ya bag anything this morning?* And one of the men yelled, *Not yet. Can I get a tin and did you catch that girl from Coal City on the Voice last night, singing Prine? I bout cried through the whole damn thing. They never show us like that on television.*

Tonight I'm doing another reading in the Northeast, and the person who is hosting is not interested in me being there. And it's fine. I get it. She doesn't know where I went to school or where I was born or that we probably had a similar upbringing. She doesn't know anything about me, other than I'm the guy who writes the poems about West Virginia and football and how people put orcas in tiny pools to watch them perform tricks. How nothing majestic should be caged for another's entertainment. I've met hundreds of these kinds of people. She talks of safe spaces at the Ivy League school she works at, and queer folks and Black folks and she says *folks* and she says how people in the South are endangering lives and looks at me when she says *South*, as if I'd spent my whole life in the South or any of my life in the South, as if queer people do not live in the South, as if Black people do not live in the South, as if queer Black people do not live in the South, as if diversity is somehow excluded from being rural, as if Appalachia and the South are the same thing, as if I was the living, breathing embodiment of everything against progress and liberalism because through the lens of football and my grandmother and the way people treat orcas I came to understand America. As if because I simply believe that regardless of where a person is born and how they speak, that they are still people, complex and flawed, but people just the same. And then to avoid screwing up the pronouns of the readers, she instead said *y'all,* remarking, *Isn't this gender nonconforming pronoun beautiful?* as if it couldn't have been beautiful because it came from one of us. As if it wasn't beautiful when my great uncle whose dad ate a whole un-peeled banana on the boat that brought him to this country, who thought baseball and the Yankees were what it was to be an American, grew up to be one of the best pitchers in the history of West Virginia. After signing his contract with the Yankees, my great uncle Joe spent part of his signing bonus on the first washer and dryer my grandma ever owned. And clear as day I can imagine my grandma standing in the yard, pulling clothing from the line. The clothing of the children and men she looked after. Her back to the street as her three young boys ran about her legs like a racetrack and my great uncle Joe walking up from the street, yelling, *Y'all won't have to do the wash by hand anymore,* the most beautiful sentence ever spoken.

*another thing i wonder about while
my father is lost at sea*

....

Can my father even sail?

One Fourth of July when I was eleven, my father and I went sailing together to see fireworks over Long Beach, about a half mile off the coast and only seven or so miles away from where the boat was docked in Newport. This was the only time I'd ever been sailing with him.

Let's keep in mind that the Pacific Ocean was named in 1520 by explorer Ferdinand Magellan. Now that guy was a real sailor. He was Portuguese and yet managed to get the Spanish crown to pay him to explore the oceans of the world. And after sailing around South America in a body of water called the Caribbean and then the South Atlantic, he turned westward through a strait and said, *LOOK AT THIS. LOOK at this waterway*, but of course he said it in Portuguese and then did the most Spanish thing ever and named that strait after himself. Then he kept going. He found himself sailing in a new body of water and he said, *Damn, this ocean is peaceful. Calm. What a quiet itty-bitty ocean.* He said, *I'll name this cute little ocean peaceful sea.* Which was also such a Spanish thing to do.

My father and I only made it five miles up the coast in the *peaceful sea* before we were stranded. We were then rescued and towed in by harbor patrol after bobbing in the Pacific for hours.

not long ago, i'd gone to a class in west virginia

....

to talk about poems. I'm sure some kids were like, *yuck*. But everyone was real nice.

I read poems about West Virginia and my grandma. I talked about music. I told them how I love football. Some of them wore sweaters with names of prestigious universities. Some were dressed like they just got out of a Cabela's. Some looked like they were on a fashion blog and some looked like me. But all these kids were different and beautiful and I wanted to tell them they could be anything they wanted.

Many times when I get asked to talk to West Virginia kids, it's to inspire them. Sometimes people want me to tell them that there is a bigger world than the one they come from. Sometimes it's to tell them that no matter what the television says, no matter what the internet says, that they are no different from any other kids around the country. As I drove all the way back through Maryland and Pennsylvania and New Jersey to New York, I thought about all the things I wish I told them that I didn't.

So I wrote a poem for all them.

....

High School Commencement Speech for West Virginia Kids

Some of you are thinking, *I've got to get out of here as fast as I can*

    and that's okay.

Some of you are thinking, *I can't imagine living in a world that is not here*

    and that's okay too.

Some of you are gonna travel far, far away and fall in love with your new home

    and that's okay.

Some of you will stay and want nothing more than to live there

    and that's okay too.

Some of you, after being so far away, will say, *I want to come home, I miss the mountains and rivers, the way a syllable rolls off the tongue there, and I want to bring parts of this other place with me*

    and that's okay.

Some of you will say I'm never going back there

    and that's okay too.

Some of you will come back and be deterred by the politics and government here and leave again and some of you will stay and fight and either way

    that's okay.

It's all okay, so long as when you leave you don't try to lose your accent because of what others say. Don't forget to eat a pepperoni roll for me. Don't forget people don't build fences between their houses here, and trains still pass each night moving bits of the state somewhere else, *that you are this state's most important resource*, as long as you don't fear who you are because of this place,

   then it's all okay.

Some people will be mad that you don't come back and they will call you all sorts of things, but as long as you have your reasons,

   then that's okay.

You won't be able to fix everything. You won't be able to know without listening, so don't forget to listen. Don't forget on the hard days that you are of the place of Bill Withers and of Katherine Johnson, who sat at a kitchen table learning to calculate the distance between Charleston and the moon. Don't forget Jennifer Garner grew up here, that you can be successful away from here and still be madly in love with it. Don't forget Henry Louis Gates is from here and Daniel Johnson and Don Knotts, and Gilligan from *Gilligan's Island* loved it here too. Don't forget Randy Moss. Don't forget the names of all people you love too.

Don't forget wherever you are to leave a porch light on for me, to never stop growing.

If you want to change your home, it helps to go out into the world and see how others are doing it. If you want to change the world, become a teacher or a nurse. Make sure to look after others.

The Mothman will still be here when you get back.

If you're coming back through, don't forget that this place is as good as any to wish upon.

my mother is speaking in a voice,
but it's not my mother's voice

....

She's held back this voice from me, until now. This kind of worry is unprecedented to me because she is the parent and I'm the kid and I'm never supposed to hear her like this.

"I just don't know what to do."

"Yeah?"

"You know your sister wrote your dad a long email before he left asking him not to go." Now I feel a little bad for not doing more.

"So how long has he been missing?" I ask.

"They set sail Friday night. We haven't heard from him since Sunday morning."

Today's Wednesday. Shit.

"You know our whole marriage he's never gone a whole day without calling me," and she pauses a moment. My mother is the kind of person who thinks about what she says before she says it. "Yeah. I just don't know what to do," she says.

I put on my best voice. The one I use when I have to be in front of people. The one that inspires confidence. The one where I pretend I know what I'm doing. The one I've been learning all these years. The voice I use when people ask, *How is your writing going?* and even though my stomach hurts because I'm hungry and even though I'm lost, with that voice I answer *great.* And I use that voice and I say: "Well, knowing him, if there were instructions for that satellite phone, he didn't read them. There's probably something he hasn't figured out."

"Ha. I never thought about that. You know, you're probably right," she says. "You know the last time he and I talked they were already running low on fuel."

"Day two of an eleven-day voyage?" I say, sarcastically, instead of all the kinds of things my mother needs me to say. But she laughs.

"But we just have to try something."

AND I realize in that moment, that I've never seen my parents' marriage so strong. That my mom really misses my dad, and so I swallow my original tactic and say, "Mom, he's going to be okay. He's the luckiest man I know. He's gonna get home safe. He's done things way more dumb than this and gotten home okay."

And that's what growing up is all about, I think, when I get off the phone. More than anything else, it's about using a particular voice to convince your mother that your father who went to Panama to sail the Caribbean Blue, against all odds, is going to get home safe.

....

A couple hours later my mom says, "Just got off the phone with Grandpa and he says you have to be on the deck to get a connection." And though I was just guessing, it was good to see my mother's worry taper a bit. My mother's father sailed and has been around boats. My mom grew up with boats and it's strange my dad asked neither of them about what to do before leaving.

"See? He probably just doesn't know how to use his phone," I say.

My sister calls later that day.

"Do you think Dad is gonna make it back?"

"I have no idea," I say.

She starts crying on the phone and I realize I've taken the wrong approach with her. And even though she's in California and I'm in New York City, I can see her in the room with me. Only it's not her. It's a younger version of her from middle school or high school. It's the version of my little sister that I left when I turned eighteen and she was twelve. It was my little sister from the time my dad took us to McDonald's, when we were really, really young and she and I were in the ball pit that smelled like piss and a boy about my age did something to make her cry and she left the pit and I left with her and she cried to my dad and I didn't want her to cry and so I said, "Dad, this kid made Paige cry," and he said, "What are you doing telling me about it? You should have knocked the crap out of the kid. You're supposed to stand up for your sister."

My sister is smarter than me. She was better at school than me. She's always had more friends than me. Had I been around when she was in high school, who knows what I would have done to some of those kids.

Though, maybe I would have cowered. I know the

difference between bravery and acting on impulse, and seldom have I ever done the brave thing when given a second to consider the consequences of bravery.

On the phone I'm listening to the version of my sister that told me about all the things that happened to her in high school and I wish I could have been there to do something, because I didn't want her to have to swallow any of what I went through, and here I was letting her down again.

The thing about growing up and making decisions is I can do it from time to time, but I know I'm not nearly consistent enough to be any good for anyone else. I have good intentions but I can't always get my actions to match them. I often think people mean well but consistency in our actions is difficult, because we are all dealing with so much on a given day. I couldn't even manage to carry over a brave voice from one phone conversation to the next.

So I say, "I'm just kidding. Of course he's coming back."

"We called the coast guard," she says.

"Oh. Well, I'm sure they will find him. How's work?"

"Well, I mean we called the coast guard in Florida, hoping they would talk to the authorities in Panama and Nicaragua. It's busy without Dad here. People aren't listening to me, because he's not here."

"Tell them to go fuck themselves. You're going to be running that place someday."

"Yeah?"

"Yeah. And say it just like that: *Go fuck yourself.* Yeah. Dad's gonna be alright and you are gonna be alright and we are both going to come home soon."

But of course, nothing was alright.

....

Each morning I sneak out of the apartment. I walk around the neighborhood. I go sit in a pew at St. John the Divine. It's not even a Catholic church and while brand is usually important in American superstition, at a time like this I guess it doesn't matter. I don't pray. I just sit and look up at the long organ pipes. I look at all the old stones. I watch an elderly couple walk past me. I say, *Dad, you better come home.* I cross myself and walk back to the apartment.

In the apartment I sit at the table near a window that over-looks the Hudson. I watch all the tiny boats float by. My girl-friend asks, *Have you heard anything new?* and her mother asks, *Heard anything new?* and her father asks, *Hear anything about your father?* And I say, *No. No. No.*

....

My mother calls again. She's been on the phone with all kinds of people over the last few days: her parents, her friends, the authorities, people she hasn't talked to in years. Anyone that will listen.

"Mom, I think it's just that he doesn't know how to use his phone."

I've said it so many times, I'm starting to believe it too.

i don't think he knows how to
use his phone

....

I tell my girlfriend's father.

"Isn't your dad an engineer?"

"Yeah, but not like that kind of engineer."

I break down in the kitchen to my girlfriend's father. "I'm worried," I say. "My dad doesn't know how to sail." I tell him how the last time my father spoke to my mother, he said they were sailing in eighteen-hour shifts and he wasn't able to sleep because of the rocking and he was too big for the bed. I tell him my dad had no idea what he was getting himself into. I tell him that my dad calls it the Caribbean Blue and that there's not much difference between an ocean and a sea. I tell him how many people drowned in a kiddy pool this year.

The kitchen is the kitchen but also his office. It's very narrow and when more than one person is inside, you almost have to dance with each other to find your way through.

So we dance.

Then we make ourselves a drink and we turn his computer speakers on real loud and we start going through the history of Bob Dylan together, which is what we do when we're down.

I tell him how much I love the song *It's All Over Now, Baby Blue* and pull up the video where Bob sings it to Donovan in a hotel room. I tell him it was in that moment that I learned that the proficiency of a musician and singer is never as important as the spirit and that sometimes in music and art, when the spirit of the thing creates meaning, the numinous trance of it is more important and more beautiful than getting it perfect. And I show him a video of Bob Dylan playing that song at the Newport Folk Festival because people demanded he play acoustic music. I tell him how he was singing it to all these people so he could say goodbye because as he walked off the stage, he was new. He was a new person.

My girlfriend's dad asks me if I know what the words to another Dylan song mean, and I say no. I say like prayers sometimes it's not just about the meaning of a singular word or phrase, but the cadences we use to trick our minds to subvert our reality. If you say it enough or sing it right, a word takes on new meaning. I say not every beautiful or brilliant thing has to be a metaphor for something else. The sound of something can be beautiful too. Beauty can make meaning, where before linear meaning didn't exist.

He then talks about being young in Greece and listening to Leonard Cohen and floating in the Aegean Sea and how he could see all the stars when he looked up at night.

"Do you miss Greece?"

"I miss the food. I miss the greens I can't get here. Women used to sell these dandelion greens on the side of the road after the war. They're one of the things I miss."

So I tell him how my grandma used to make me pepperoni rolls. When I was young she'd ship them to California and I'd write her letters and that's how I started writing. I tell him how we forced her to retire from making pepperoni rolls a few years back when she stuffed them with as much plastic as pepperoni. I tell him how we used to tailgate with our family before football games in my grandpa's old office. And how our family would come in from all over in those days and my grandpa's office was only a short walk from the stadium. My cousins from Elkins would bring venison and my cousins from Bridgeport would bring venison and my cousins from

Parkersburg would bring venison and apple and black walnut pie. "They did all kinds of things to those deer," I say. There was venison jerky, venison stew, venison burgers, venison chili, venison kebabs, venison soup, venison stir-fry, venison lasagna, spaghetti and venison meatballs, venison pot roast, and if you could think it up they had a venison version. I tell him that it's because we always ate and drank so well before these games that I often misconstrue football with the act of a Sunday family dinner or some gathering with religious or holiday implications. There was always enough to eat and drink and a story to be told. There was always laughter. I tell him how when I found out I couldn't eat gluten anymore, how buckwheat pancakes became my weekend staple and reminded me of falls in Preston County at the buckwheat festival filled with buckwheat pancakes, sausage patties, roaming livestock auctions and gigantic hot-air balloons that painted the sky like fall leaves. I tell him how not long after I got sick, I moved back to West Virginia to write a book, how I got a little poor and a little skinny and some women I taught writing to started cooking for me so I could eat a nice meal during our classes and they'd load me up with enough leftovers to last me all week. I tell him about how this is where I first learned about the ramp, a West Virginia root that's garlicky and pretty much makes everything taste better. I tell him how food has always transported me back to Appalachia and sometimes I'll be in a restaurant in New York City and I'll see traces of Appalachia. But whatever stroke of it they use, it never feels quite the thing that makes it taste like home. It's always lacking community.

There's something to catching up in the kitchen with my grandma and grandpa when I was young and catching up over hot dogs and venison and pie and there was something about being fed by people who though may never have said, "Keegan, I love you," showed it to me with their cooking. I tell him how Appalachian food is as much about what is being eaten as it is the people you share your food with. I tell him how when I get together each summer with my friends, who've now mostly scattered around the state and beyond, I look forward most to when we cook these large family-style dinners and breakfasts. How we all get to eat fresh food from the gardens of our families, from the same gardens our families used to sprout us up, and how my friends are the ones continuing this tradition. I tell him how sometimes we get a little tipsy and sing and dance a whole bunch in whichever kitchen we're in. How someone is always looking on in astonishment at the time we're all having, and someone's mom and dad are always getting in on the dancing and all of us are telling each other the stories of our goings-on and all that lives in all the breaths between these meals. I tell him when I think of Appalachian food, I think of home. I tell him how whenever I feel lost and distant, when I'm trying to explain to strangers what makes West Virginia so special to me, there's this untranslatable moment that can't fully be recognized unless you go there and seek it out yourself. And so when I talk of pepperoni rolls, and hot dogs and chili and ramps, there are people who get it and people who don't. They understand that it's about the hands that make the rolls and about the words we use while we eat the rolls, and it's about how together in this community our hearts are able to live on in spite of everything.

....

I start googling maps of the Caribbean, which is not a good idea.

I realize my father is taking the worst possible route. Instead of hopping islands, he headed south. Unless he's hugging the Central American Coast, he's in the middle of a giant body of water with no land around for hundreds of miles. Thanks to the internet I realize I may never see my father again.

....

A few mornings later, before I can sneak out to go not pray at the cathedral, my girlfriend's father offers to cook me breakfast.

"Alright," I say. I look out the window at the Hudson and watch boats float by.

A little while later he returns with eggs and bacon and potatoes dressed up with ramps.

"Look what I found on my walk yesterday," he says. "I just hope I cooked them right."

Surprising me with ramps was an Appalachian act because at its core it was an act of love. For the first time in a long while, something tasted like home.

one day while i was on tour, my friend bryan, who's super into ghost stories, the occult, metal music, and zines, says

....

"Have you heard of the WVU Coed Murder podcast?"
"No."
"You should check it out."

So I check it out so I will have something to do to avoid thinking about my dad being lost in the middle of the Caribbean Sea. But I just can't stop thinking of my dad.

According to the podcast, when my dad was sixteen he was growing up in a different West Virginia than the West Virginia I know today. He never told me any of this. There weren't highways yet in the early 1970s. Every road was a winding road that was sometimes paved and all the roads choked mountains like a coiled snake. No one built highways unless it was to transport coal somewhere quicker. People in those days were not as important as coal. Now my cousins and uncles and aunts always say, *The most important resource in West Virginia is its people*, so no one forgets.

Back then, people hitchhiked all the time. My dad used to love to hitchhike.

My dad doesn't talk much about being young though. Other people told me he spent much of the time in the woods collecting rocks and Grandma said, "He was always sneaking people into the house who did not have a place to stay. Sometimes it was a friend and sometimes it was a homeless person." She said, "We stopped buying your dad new shoes because he'd just go up route seven and give them away to someone that needed them more. And if you're not careful, you'll turn out to be a little Communist just like him."

My dad doesn't talk much about it, so I've always imagined his Morgantown to be not all that dissimilar from the Morgantown I know. But apparently that's not true at all.

ONE NIGHT when my dad was sixteen and God knows where he was, it started snowing.

The snow started coming down in thick sheets as two women were leaving the Metropolitan Theater after a movie. The theater sits on High Street, and my dad lived on South High Street which is the same street just on the other side of a short bridge.

If you had good enough eyes and there wasn't so much snow and you happened to be standing in front of his house, there's a chance theoretically you could have seen the two coeds on the sidewalk in front of the theater from his childhood home. That's how close the theater was to my father's house.

And the snow was really coming down that night. It gets so cold in Morgantown because the downtown is wedged in a valley of lazy sloping hills and the banks of the Monongahela River run alongside it. Sometimes weather has trouble passing over the hills and sometimes weather clouds get stuck above the town. The exposed rock in the side of those hills and the river do wonders to keep the cold in. The river flows north. People always say, *This is the only river in the whole world that flows north other than the Amazon River*, but that's not true at all. People have been telling me this my whole life, but apparently many rivers flow north and I wonder why people say such things. I wonder if they felt the grandeur of Morgantown needed a comparison to the exotic jungles of the Amazon so people would understand.

I've always thought Morgantown was wild and beautiful and grand all by itself.

And I'm sure as the two shivering women left that movie theater and looked up at the snow falling, which would have been lit up by the lampposts they were under, that they could see all kinds of colors in the snow's crystals. I'm sure that the lamplight would have made the snow look like diamonds falling all around them.

The two girls were freshmen at West Virginia University and one was named Mared and the other Karen. They must have been real cold because they looked all around them at the snow and streets and at the snow all about them again and decided to hitchhike less than a mile back to their dorms. They were seen getting into a cream-colored Chevy with a man who looked to be in his forties.

They were never seen again.

Well, that's not totally true. They were never seen alive with their heads strapped on to their bodies again, is what I mean.

It would have been in all the papers then. Police from all over the state were searching for these two women. There was a $3,500 reward so everyone started giving tips. Even a chapter of a cult just over the border in Maryland got in on it. And now I wonder why my dad never talked about the religious cult over the border in Maryland.

The tips were all largely hearsay. The problem was in a town that small, everything is bound to be hearsay.

The cops were acting like cops and screwed up the investigation every step of the way. In the 1970s, if you wanted to get away with murder, Morgantown, West Virginia, would have been a great place for that. None of the police departments shared information then. You could just kill someone and drive over the county line and no one would know. Or someone would know but wouldn't tell anyone. It was like the Wild West and my dad was smack right in the middle.

Now the town is full of shops and coffee shops and artisanal donuts and restaurants and fancy beer places and screen-printing shops, but back then it was more like a bus stop on a map, which happened to have a theater and a university and a couple churches and college basketball and football teams.

It was apparently a great place to throw parties and commit murder in the seventies. Of course my dad never told me any of this, because he never talks to me about anything.

Then one day the police received an anonymous letter from God knows who, and it had all these geometry terms in it and was written in a very eloquent voice, the kind of voice you don't trust, ever. Everyone knows that the person who writes out *sir* or *madam* in a letter is of course *the person* who's capable of killing someone. The letter did say the person writing the letter would reveal themselves when the bodies were found. The bodies were not found until much, much later.

A second letter was received by the police. The second letter used the same geometry terms and eloquent voice, but try as they did, the police were terrible at scavenger hunts for bodies. A third letter was sent and this time the national guard was called in and they were much better at finding bodies.

To be fair though, the tips weren't really directions and could have sent the searchers in one of a million directions depending on where they decided to leave from. But because the bodies were found, everyone thought the tips were real. I would say it was more coincidence and trial and error than anything. Like if you were looking for your lost Twinkie and I said, *Look in the southern most north northwest quadrant of your kitchen,* and after three or four times of saying this you found your lost Twinkie, I would be no hero.

Of course this wasn't a Twinkie people were searching for.

When the bodies were discovered, they were in a kind of tomb beneath some stones and tree limbs and an officer at some point said, "Wow. If I'd just been walking around out here I'd never had seen the bodies," which means it was an extra good thing that the national guard was there and another example of how terrible the police are at scavenger hunts.

When the bodies were discovered, they were badly decomposed and also headless. *What happened to the heads?* people wondered for years. The letter writer never revealed their identity, because they never do. People chalked it up to the occult and case was closed.

Then a little while later people said, *You can't keep blaming things on people who think they have magic powers, especially if they don't have magic powers. These people likely couldn't carry this out, especially being that they have no magic powers.*

After that a man confessed. But it was a forced confession of sorts. He fit the profile and had been known to decapitate too. Well, sorta. That's what people thought. He was more of a murderer than a decapitator. He'd killed a bunch of people all up and down the East Coast, but never really decapitated anyone. He later used this killing in testimony, hoping that by using this murder in West Virginia he could prove he couldn't have murdered the people he murdered in the murder trial he was currently on trial for. After that trial, which he got off scot-free from, unbeknownst to him, he got sent to West Virginia to be tried for this murder. In those days extradition was weird, but no one seemed to have a problem with putting a known murderer on trial for a murder he confessed to. Of course he admitted that he didn't really kill these two women later and that he read about the killings in a magazine and was playing his odds of getting off through an incredibly basic understanding of double jeopardy, which wasn't really even double jeopardy. And of course there wasn't enough evidence to rightfully convict him because he probably didn't kill the women.

But he was convicted anyway.

You just can't go around talking about murdering women in West Virginia without facing consequences. And he faced them.

That weird little murderer died in prison, innocent of this crime and most everyone knew it.

Also, this podcast taught me that there was a ton of murder in the United States in the 1970s. I wonder why my dad never told me about that.

Once it was obvious that this man could not have killed these women—and after he had died in prison, where he atoned for his previous sins—people got to talking.

"That weird little man probably didn't do it," people said. "That means the real killer could still just be walking around town."

It's rumored that in the years after the murder there were at least seven potential suspects just walking around the area who easily could have committed the murder. One of the problems with the trial was that there were maybe too many suspects to choose from. People who had probably maybe murdered someone else too, but were never tried, just walked around, maybe murdering other people.

During that time no one went into West Virginia unless you were going to play football or basketball and the only thing that left the state was coal and timber. It was a pretty good place for people on the lam, hiding secrets and dead people if they needed to hide secrets or people. But then there were also suspects from around town too. There was an elected official with ties to the mob who may or may not been having an affair with one of the girls. There was a dentist who had been molesting women he put under and who my dad may have even gone to as a boy. One of the victims had an appointment with him the day she disappeared, but she didn't show up for her appointment.

And I wonder why my dad never told me about any of those people lurking around town when he was a boy.

According to the podcast, the gruesome nature of the killings exacerbated stereotypes commonly held of West Virginians at the time.

I WONDER about my father in the woods collecting rocks and my father hitchhiking out of town to get to where the good rock lay. I wonder if my dad saw the two women the night they were kidnapped, if he might have stumbled past their bodies without knowing it while searching for rocks or if he stumbled upon those bodies and was too afraid to tell anyone. I wonder if the newspaper headlines gave him bad dreams at night or if just overhearing what people murmured in town gave him bad dreams. I wonder what it was like to live in a place where so many evil people lived that you could not, without a reasonable doubt, whittle down a list of possible murder suspects, for a murder where two women were beheaded, to a handful of suspects. I wonder if that place is everywhere.

I wonder if he was terrified. Perhaps he wasn't. He's Big Joe after all. I wonder if that night he was drinking with some friends not knowing that any of this was possible, not knowing people could live in a world where they could be drinking some beer and listening to Bob Seger and across the way another person could be cutting the heads off of women. I wonder what waking up the next day was like. I wonder if he was thinking, *I want to get out of this town and start new* or if he was thinking about the rocks he collected and the changing seasons he'd miss. I wonder if he was dreaming of going to France then. I wonder why he never told me about these murders and all these dangerous people he lived among as a child.

I WONDER if he left on a sailboat looking for the words to tell me such things someday, that maybe no place is safe, not even the place that lives in our hearts. If my dad makes it home alive, I know the first thing I'll say to him. I'll say, "Dad, why'd you never tell me of those two WVU coeds that got kidnapped and got their heads chopped off just a couple blocks away from Grandma's house?"

....

But that's not what I said.

....

"Your dad finally called me," my mom says.

When she says *your dad,* it sounds like the word *dad* and not like that word at all. It's something else. It feels new. It feels like a dream right before you wake.

"Your dad said after they ran out of most of their gas they couldn't use the generator to charge his phone and so he couldn't call or receive calls. Their sail tore and the other guy had to sew it back together using a giant needle and his hands were bleeding all over the deck and into the ocean. Your dad couldn't get any sleep and the other guys were partying the whole time and were not exactly capable of sailing." She says, "They're going to shoot for Jamaica now and when your dad makes landfall he's gonna fly home. I have to get off so I can call everyone back now."

I TRY calling my dad that night, but I don't get through. I leave a voicemail. I say: *Dad, come home. As soon as you get to Jamaica, fly home. Don't keep on to Cuba or the Keys. Paige needs you. Mom needs you. I need you. Don't you ever do anything this stupid ever again. Just get your ass home. I'm glad you're safe. I don't know what I was going to do without you. I love you. Call me when you can.*

Then there is a woman's voice giving me directions on how to make sure this voicemail gets to my father and I hit the wrong button and *poof* my message is erased.

I call again that night and nothing. I wake the next day and call. Nothing. Call at lunch. Nothing. He's able to talk to my mom and my sister, and they both needed that and so I am glad.

MY MOM calls me the next afternoon.

"They have this little dog on the boat too," she says. "And it was crapping everywhere and the boat's bathroom broke."

And then my sister calls me and tells me about how my dad had to shower using salt water and that after they ran out of gas, they couldn't run their generator. She says because their fridge ran off their generator they weren't able to keep it on and most of their food spoiled and they had to throw it overboard. She says that my father said they brought more beer than water and only enough water for seven days and have been out for fifteen. She says that he told her it was the first time he'd been scared for his life.

....

Five days later I get another text from my mother:

Dad got rescued by a Filipino tanker. I guess they got there before the coastguard did. I'm gonna go on Facebook and tell everyone. I have to call people!

Alright! I text back.

THE NEXT day I look at Facebook and sure enough there's my dad. And he's alive. There's pictures on the *Filipino* freighter of the bunk bed he's sleeping in with a caption: *best night sleep ever.* There are pictures of bottles of hot sauce in a mess hall captioned: *love this food. Could get used to this.* There was a picture of my dad looking much thinner, with tan arms and tired eyes and white facial hair and never in my life before that moment, before staring into a computer screen at a picture of my father who was thousands of miles away, had I ever seen my father with any kind of facial hair other than his pepper and salt mustache. He had a white beard now. He was surrounded by a couple Filipino men who were part of the freighter crew. One crew member was smiling and had his arm raised up, giving the rock out sign. There was my dad's crew too. One guy, the one who knew what he was doing, with his arm all gauzed up and the other guy, the captain, looking drunk behind them. My dad's expression looks like he's screaming *woooooooooooooooooo.*

And I hope he is.

....

When my dad finally calls me he sounds nothing like the *wooooooooooooooooo* picture.

But I guess the internet can be misleading that way. He called while I was walking along the High Line in New York with my girlfriend, basking in the first day of summer. It was the first time I'd heard from him in weeks. "I'm just glad you didn't come," he says. "I knew the second I saw the boat."

He pauses for a moment. The way a person who has something important to say pauses before continuing. The way a person who has experienced something searches for the right and exact words before choosing, because they want their experience to translate.

"There was dog crap everywhere." He pauses again. "But I just couldn't back out on them. I lost track of the time because we were doing these long shifts and after the sail tore, we'd lost all our food and the only thing I had in the whole world was this bag of beef jerky. I hid that bag from the others. And I don't feel bad at all about it. The dog kept trying to get near me 'cause he could smell it on me, and I thought this might be the only thing I'd ever eat again and so I kept it hidden. I thought I may never eat real food again," he says.

"Wow," I say.

"Then the propeller broke and fell off. Lucky for us the other guy was able to dive down into the ocean and find it and put it back on. He was the only one that knew what he was doing. And I never could get to sleep and so after a few days it was hard to tell how much time was passing and if it was passing at all and I just didn't understand time anymore. And I was hungry and tired. But there was this one night. This one night where the moon was out. And all the ocean all around us was lit up by the moon. And there was this group of dolphins. Hundreds of them. And it was the most beautiful thing I'd ever seen. I thought it was a sign. I knew this whole thing was going to turn around. And it was as if they were following us that night, protecting us. And the next day we got rescued by a Filipino tanker and the captain of the tanker said he'd never before rescued anyone and it was his last voyage ever. And the first bite of the Filipino food, man. It was so good. I thought I was in heaven. But those dolphins, buddy, I wish you could have seen those dolphins."

AND FOR a moment, through the scratchy reception of the satellite phone, I consider that my dad both knows everything and nothing at all. I consider we all know everything and nothing at all. I think on all the things someone does to show you they have a few poems tucked inside themselves somewhere.

. . . .

That night I went to bed before learning all the details of the trip. Before I had every explanation for the gaps in narrative, before I discovered why they chose the route they took, why they only brought eleven cases of water, and I was able to fall asleep peacefully.

With my eyes closed I could see ocean and moon. A tiny sailboat with a torn sail and a broken propeller. Three men and a small pug, all lost together in that ocean. And then dolphin. Dolphin. Dolphin, dolphin, dolphin blooming from the moonlight, the only thing for hundreds of miles, pointing toward wherever home may be.

father's day

....

A few weeks later it's Father's Day and I'm back on the road again. And what they don't tell you about this life is that you can be in a room full of people and still feel lonely. You can be in a van full of people and loneliness will still creep up on you.

I'm no good with people anymore and I'm lonely all the time, but my dad is safe and so I walk a little lighter. I walk a little lighter out the venue I just read at and my phone rings and I see it's a call from him. He sent a picture of him and my sister and my mother together drinking drinks out of tall glasses with straws that loop, from the balcony of some fancy hotel on a beach a couple miles from where I grew up. You can probably see the power plant from their balcony.

My dad once took me up the top of that power plant not knowing how scared of heights I was. You could see the whole world from up there. From up there I could feel the world's curvature. I thought I was gonna puke.

They can probably see the white clouds the power plant is puffing into the sky from its smokestack fingers and the trailer park that sits next to the power plant. They can see the ocean from there too and an island off the coast called Catalina where some John Wayne movies were filmed. I guess to make the films seem more real, someone brought buffalo to that island and just left them there and now buffalo freely roam on an island off the coast of California. And sometimes in life things happen that change the context for everything we use to understand life around us.

My dad starts telling his story about his sailing adventure to anyone who will listen and new things come out every time he tells it. My mom about has a heart attack every time he tells it but he keeps on telling it anyway. He tells it to his friends and strangers, to anyone who will listen.

Maybe sometimes you have to be so close to death to have a story worth telling for your life to mean something to yourself. Maybe you have to be so close to death and then people will listen to the story you've been trying to tell them your whole life about everything that isn't death.

"HOW'S EVERYTHING, buddy?" my dad says.

"Ah, good. Just finished my set. Happy Father's Day."

"We sure wish you could be here."

"Me too."

"If you could see how beautiful this sky is, and all the colors in the sunset, you'd just love it."

"I know I would, dad. I wish I was there with you too."

I'M VERY tired and my skin is burnt from sitting in a van and walking around and swimming in lakes. People in Charleston keep telling us their secrets. The show was good but people are tired and their skin is burnt and we never get to be off-stage anymore. I've told no one that my father just got home a week ago or that he was lost at sea because what good would that do?

....

A few weeks later I'm back in New York City in the child-hood bedroom of my girlfriend in her childhood bed and I get a phone call. It's my mother.

"The sailboat sank."

"What?"

"I guess after your dad left and the other guy left, your father paid for the boat to get repaired. A few weeks later the captain tried to go out again and tried to make it to Key West. They got caught in a storm and the ship that tried to rescue them was too big. It was the size of five football fields. It made waves in the ocean and the sailboat could not stay even with the freighter and at some point the ship crashed into the sail-boat and the boat split into two and the mast came undone and the captain was in an unfortunate place and the mast took his head off. There was a Jamaican man on the boat who helped repair it in Jamaica and he has twelve children, and needed the money so he was gonna help the captain get to Key West and was able to grab the pug and jump out into the sea before anything hurt him. The ocean was tumbling because this was all during a storm and the big boat left because the boat crew was afraid of causing any more damage and the coast guard came the next day and it was just this Jamaican man and a pug floating out in the ocean and the dead headless captain."

....

After the captain died, my dad stopped telling his story so much. And even though it scared the bejesus out of my mom and me, I sometimes wish he'd tell it again.

After that, he got real sad again and turned inward. I'm not sure what he learned from the experience, or if we are always supposed to learn something when we merely survive trauma. But he's still the luckiest person I know.

"He's so quiet these days," my mother said.

"Dad's hardly yelling at anyone at work," my sister said and I knew then something must be wrong, so I decided this would be a good time to come for a visit.

A few days later I hopped onto another plane and flew three thousand miles across the plains and mountains and the entire wingspan of the continent in only five and a half hours.

I should be doing this more, I thought, somewhere over Colorado.

I DRANK before I got on the plane because I wasn't sure what I'd find when I got off. And I drank on the plane because the person next to me would not stop talking to me about an idea they had for a television show. And I drank when I got off the plane because it looked like my dad needed a drink. We went and had tacos and drank some more as one sport season was ending and another beginning on the television in front of us, in a bar dressed up in a tiki costume. As John Fogerty complained over a loudspeaker about not being put into a baseball game, my father and I said nothing to each other. We just sat in the warmth of each other's existence, which felt like enough.

It was enough just to be in the same room.

Then we went home and had a drink with my mother.

home

....

There are many things I don't know and the number of things
I don't know is a number that grows each day. It grows thick
like a forest.

My mother and I are in the kitchen and it's almost fall now
and the sky outside is turning inky. The sun is setting and the
birds are all tucked away and quiet.

"It hurts me, you know, when I read all these things and
people thinking you're from West Virginia. Why don't you
tell them you're from here," she says.

"I don't know."

"People must think you had a real terrible childhood or
bad mother."

"Nah. No one thinks that. I guess I didn't think about it
like that. But I know everyone reading these things will know.
They will all know that I have a wonderful mother."

Sometimes we have to make homes for ourselves, but my
mom will always be my mom.

Sometimes I wonder about the younger boy who would lie
in his bed each night saying over and over, *If I could just get
to West Virginia, everything would be fine.* I wonder about
the child I was, wishing each night to escape. Now I'm not
even sure what I was trying to escape in the first place. Older,
I feel ashamed of that thought. I feel ashamed of the idea of

needing to escape, especially now that my parents are older and my sister is grown, largely without me.

How do you explain you weren't trying to escape your family but all the things shriveling up around you. I was trying to escape my fear of not being able to see myself in anything around me.

But I'm of the Pacific. I hear it calling me back from time to time, and I don't know if I'll ever be allowed back, but I hear it at night when everyone's gone to sleep, when everyone thinks *no one else could be up at this hour.* I'm up at this hour, thinking about the Pacific and my sister and mother and father.

. . . .

And then I left again. I had to.

Last night while tucked away in the twin bed I share in New York City I had a dream.

I TOUCH the streetlight across the street from the Pacific Ocean. The bougainvillea mixes with the beach shrubs thumbing up out of the sand. The gulls are helium balloons overhead. The sand pipers are tracing the hard-pack sand with their needle bills. There are a few stray dogs on the beach who can't keep themselves from looking like they're smiling at each other as their owners, a quarter mile or so down the beach, make their slow stroll toward them.

Everyone is moving in slow motion.

I turn around and cross the Pacific Coast Highway, heading back to my parents' house. There are royal palm trees swaying back and forth, used as a median to separate the cars driving in different directions. There are rose beds and rectangles of lush grass and birds of paradise on one side of the street. On the other, oil pumps and arid brush. In the dream, the sun drops into the ocean, turning the sky and the sky turns the world into all the colors I love. The birds flying over suburbia choke me up and all the stories of these people I haven't met, others who I left, I finally listen to.

And as I walk down the asphalt path back toward where my parents live, I hear the word in my footsteps over and over and over. I hear the word *home*.

And as the stars begin to poke their heads out into the night sky of my dream, I think of sailors and the ocean and the stars calling the sailors back home. How the stars are the original porchlight. No matter where you are, they're blinking their Morse code: *come home*.

What I know is that in the old days, hundreds of years ago, jesters and entertainers would have to travel the world to gather enough stories and insight to entertain their kingdom. I've been gone for so long collecting stories I don't know if anyone here even recognizes me anymore or recognizes that I left, that I ever existed.

In the dream I walk to my parents' house. I know my dad will be home when I get there. It will be after a long day at work and there will be a tall Coors in his hand and I will have to come up with a story to make him smile. I listen to my footsteps conjure up something that will entertain him, that will both sound familiar and foreign, and he'll have a beer in his hand then and the TV news will be on in the background because it's late June now and football and basketball season are over and we are in the quiet part of the year again.

And then I walk into the house and there's my dad on the couch. The light of the television bouncing across his face and he is so still. There are so many things bottled up in his head and in his body, but he's alive and my mother's alive and my sister's alive and I say, "Dad, what are you thinking about?" And in my dream my dad starts telling me all the things he's kept quiet, breaking the silence he's been keeping all these years, the silence that's kept his body intact, all the stories I'd never have known about had I not asked him just then.

acknowledgments

....

Versions of these stories originally appeared in *Hobart*, *Entropy Magazine, Vol. 1 Brooklyn*, and *The Travelin' Appalachians Revue's Appalachian Food Summit Zine*.

IN GRATITUDE to the following folks who've been so support-ive over the years: Rebecca Doverspike, Mary Alice, David Doc Ramblings, Rondalyn Whitney, Andrea Null, Tracy Wil-liams, Sherrie Flick, Devin Kelly, Liz Pavlovic, Eduardo C. Corral, Patty Slagel, Kayla Good, Erica Rogers, Ethel Morgan Smith, Isabelle Shepherd, Karla Hilliard, Jessica Salfia, Jessica Michael Bowman, Jesús Moya, Josh M. Tawney, Tyler and Alyssa, Christopher Jackson, Aunt Paulette and Aunt Jennifer, Carol Hamblen, Maya Bidanda, Philip Matthews, Ace Bog-gess, the West Virginia Humanities Council, Ian Axel Ander-son, Mina Bruno, Stephen Furlong, Francis and Hong, Chris Oxley, the Saley family, the Walters family, Nicholas Larson, Jon Smithers, Randi Ward, Walter Smelt, Maria Pinto, Nick Chambers, Tony Tillehkooh, Ashleigh Bryant Phillips, Chen Chen, Jeff Gilbert, Mandy Ranck, Michelle Betters, Lydia Cyrus, Torli Bush, Gregg Emery, Jaime Zuckerman, Marie Gale Thompson, Rosalio Lopez, Andrew Squitiro, Rebekah Cotton, Uncle Jimmy, Uncle Pat, Uncle Chris and Aunt Janice and Aunt Teddi, Anna Hughes, Mary Webber, the Hugheses and Jerans, Becky, Jennifer, Jeff, Jason and Aunt Barbra, Mike Costello, Crystal Good, Roger May, Jessica Riz, Scott Mc-Clanahan, Avery, Aki, Caleb, Kap, Nathan Thomas, Billy Matheny, Steven Dunn, and Savannah Sipple, and Mared & Karen: The WVU Coed Murders Podcast, 123 Pleasant Street, Kin Ship Goods, and Base Camp Printing.

Paul Miller, thank you for being my friend, through good years and bad. I wouldn't have been able to finish this without your eyes, heart, and brain, without you literally telling me over and over *finish it*.

Sally and Christos: thank you for taking me in, making sure I always had enough to eat and a winter coat when the weather turned ugly.

Renée Nicholson: you were the first teacher in my life who told me they believed in me. You're family.

Courtney, Branden, Fern, and Walden: for all times you've said *I love you*, especially the times when you didn't know how badly I needed to hear it from someone, you all are my forever home.

Lisa Stender, MJ, and Malia: international prom and our road trip to New York will always be on my mind and in my heart. Your friendship and love all these years has kept me going.

Joe Halstead: for being the truth and the first reader of this book, for teaching me to live in my own skin.

Kevin Chesser: my brilliant friend, you are the poet and person I hope to someday become.

Eva Maria Saavedra: you have been the constant and unwavering light throughout my twenties and thirties, your friendship grows more steadfast with each year.

Ashley Lester: my hero and role model and favorite triathlete, you've been one of the greatest gifts in my life.

My Trav App family whom I carry with me everywhere: Howard, Tyler, Bryan, John, Hannah, Sophia, Kelsie, Darrin, Jenn, Roseanne, and of course Betty—thank you.

Roxy Todd and Zander Aloi: thank you for mailing back my notebook after I left it at the Red Carpet in Charleston. It was the beginning of this whole book. You don't know this, but I listen to your voices on NPR when I get homesick.

Bud Smith: thank you for pulling your work truck over one day to take a call from me when we were complete strangers. Thank you for your belief in earlier versions of this work. It helped me slog through tougher parts of this journey.

Emily Sokolosky: thank you for your cover art. My apartment is filled with your prints. You designing this book cover is a dream come true.

Derek and Sarah: thank you for your guidance and support. I am so grateful for both of you.

Thank you to the entire staff at WVU Press.

Mom, Dad, Paige, and Joey: I have known unfathomable love because of you four and will always be grateful and indebted to you.

Eleni: for showing me how one ought to live, for convincing me to continue to be enchanted by all the magic in the world around me—for taking me as I am, thank you.